PENDENNIS & ST. MAWES:

AN HISTORICAL SKETCH OF TWO CORNISH CASTLES

A facsimile of the edition first published in 1875

S. PASFIELD OLIVER, F.S.A., F.R.G.S.

DYLLANSOW TRURAN

This facsimile edition of the original published by
Dyllansow Truran
Cornish Publications
Trewolsta, Trewirgie, Redruth, Cornwall

First published 1875

This edition first published 1984

Printed and bound in Great Britain by A. Wheaton & Co. Ltd., Exeter
ISBN 0 907566–90–1

PENDENNIS CASTLE.

PENDENNIS & St. MAWES:

AN HISTORICAL SKETCH OF TWO CORNISH CASTLES.

BY

S. PASFIELD OLIVER, F.S.A., F.R.G.S.,

CAPTAIN ROYAL ARTILLERY, AND CORRESPONDING MEMBER ANTHROPOLOGICAL INSTITUTE, ETC., AUTHOR OF "MADAGASCAR AND THE MALAGASSY," "LES HOVAS," "TWO ROUTES THROUGH NICARAGUA," "NURAGGHI SARDI," "MEGALITHIC STRUCTURES OF THE CHANNEL ISLANDS," "DOLMEN-MOUNDS AND AMORPHOLITHS OF BRITTANY," ETC., ETC., ETC

WITH ILLUSTRATIONS.

" Pendinas tenet asperi cacumen
Celsum montis, et intonat frequenter.
Mauditi quoque subsidet rotundum
Castrum et fulminat impetu furenti,
Portus ostia quà patent Falensis."
(Cygnea Cantio) Leland.

TRURO:
W. LAKE, PRINCES STREET.
LONDON
SIMPKIN, MARSHALL & Co., STATIONERS' HALL COURT.

1875.

W. LAKE, STEAM PRESS, TRURO.

ILLUSTRATIONS.

1.   PENDENNIS CASTLE ... ... *Frontispiece.*

2.   TURRET, PENDENNIS CASTLE ... ... *page* 1

3.   GURGOYLE, ditto 8

4.   EMBAYED WINDOW, ditto 9

5.   MAYOR'S CUP AT PENRYN 20

6.   GURGOYLE, PENDENNIS CASTLE 27

7.   ROYAL ARMS OVER ENTRANCE TO CASTLE 28

8.   ENTRANCE TO FALMOUTH HARBOUR—FROM PENDENNIS 45

9.   GURGOYLE, PENDENNIS CASTLE... 68

10.   ST. MAWES CASTLE AND HARBOUR ... ... *facing* 79

11.   GATEWAY, ST. MAWES CASTLE 79

12.   GURGOYLE, ditto 83

13.   ENTRANCE TO FALMOUTH HARBOUR—FROM ST. MAWES 91

WORKS REFERRED TO.

Boase and Courtney's Bibliotheca Cornubiensis, vol. 1. A to O. 1874.

Borlase's Antiquities of Cornwall, 1759.

Britton and Brayley's Cornwall Illustrated, 1832.

Burke's Peerage and Baronetage, 1873.

Burton's Diary, edit. 1828.

Calamy's Nonconformists Memorial, edit.
1862.

Camden's Britania, by Gibson, 1772.

Carew's Survey of Cornwall, edit. 1811.

Clarendon's History of the Rebellion,
Oxf. 1849.

Clarendon State Papers, Oxf. 1767.

Clarendon State Papers, Calendars.

Cottonian MSS.

Froude's History, 1858.

Gentleman's Magazine.

Gilbert's Parochial History of Cornwall,
1838.

Grafton's Chronicles.

Grose's Antiquities of England and Wales,
1787.

Hals' Parochial History of Cornwall, Part
II. 1719. ?

Hals' Parochial History of Cornwall, in
Gilbert's History.

Hitchins' History of Cornwall, by Drew,
1824.

Holinshed's Chronicles, 1587.

Journals of the House of Commons.

Journals of the House of Lords.

Journal of the Royal Institution of Cornwall.

The King's Collection of Maps, Drawings,
&c.

The King's Pamphlets.

Lake's, The Parochial History of Cornwall, 1868, &c.

Landsdowne MSS.

Leland's Cygnea Cantio, 1658.

Leland's Itinerary, Oxf. 1745.

Lyson's Magna Brittanica, vol. 3, 1806-22

Markham's Life of Fairfax, 1870.

Memoirs of Philip Melvill, Lieut-Gov. of
Pendennis, [1812].

Murray's Hand Book of Devon and Cornwall.

Newspapers of the year 1646.

Norden's Speculum Britanniæ Pars. 1728.

Notes and Queries.

Polwhele's History of Cornwall. 1816.

Pryce's Archæologia Cornu-Britannia,
1790.

Pryce's MSS.

Rushworth's Historical Collections.

Sprigge's Anglia Rediviva, 1647.

State Papers, Domestic Series

State Papers, Domestic Series, Calendars.

State Papers, Treasury Series, Calendars

Strickland's Lives of the Queens of England.

Tonkin's Parochial History of Cornwall,
in Gilbert's History.

Whitaker's Parochial History of Cornwall, in Gilbert's History.

To

Robert Were Fox, F.R.S.,

and his daughter, Anna Maria,

this slight token of

respect and affection

is offered by the Author.

PREFACE.

—

THE officers of a regiment like ours, which is scattered in many places about the world at one time, have opportunities, too often, perhaps, neglected, of collecting materials for the history of our various military garrisons, forts, and stations.

On inspection of the regimental list lately published of the officers of the Royal Artillery, I find that there are two hundred separate stations in which they are quartered. By this it is apparent how wide a scope for research there is now open to the regiment.

The garrison branch of the service has, however, more especial facilities in this respect: and officers detached in out of the way places, with the charge of garrisons, could not better, perhaps, beguile the long dull winter evenings, than by collecting information as to the history of their posts: and this unquestionably, however moderate the degree of interest it might possess for them, would be of great and real interest and value to the future historian.

The Royal Artillery Institution would not, in my humble opinion, be employed improperly, if it encouraged this useful exercitation in the field of history, by receiving and publishing historical monographs or sketches of the kind suggested, compiled by officers of the Royal Artillery. At present it refuses even to receive them.

Wherever I have been myself quartered, whether at home or on foreign service, I have occupied a portion of my leisure hours in collecting a few desultory notes of the locality and its associations, and these have from time to time been published.

The following slight historical sketches of two Cornish fortresses, in which I was myself quartered in the year 1873, are now offered, as a very humble example of the sort of exercise I have been recommending, and I hope it will be followed by many of my brother officers. The original sketches were read, from my MS., to a small circle of friends, headed by Miss A. M. Fox, in the castles themselves, at the conclusion of the meeting of the Cornwall Polytechnic Institution, in the autumn of 1873. They have since been completed, by the addition of a considerable amount of matter, gathered principally from the calendars of the State and Clarendon Papers, and from certain old newspapers. Not myself residing in London, with opportunities of easy access to its libraries and records, I entrusted the collection and putting into shape of this additional matter to a gentleman residing there, who has proved an able assistant, and to whom my fullest acknowledgments and best thanks are due. The names of some of the governors and lieutenant or deputy governors of the castles, with dates of their appointments, and other dates since 1754, have been supplied to me by the authorities at the war office, and I am much indebted to them for their courtesy, which will be further acknowledged at the proper places in the ensuing work.

TABLE OF CONTENTS.

PENDENNIS CASTLE.

CHAPTER I.

Pages.

Origin of name, various derivations ... ...   1—2

Pendennis a peninsula   2

Early fortifications of the promontory of Pendennis ... ...   2—3

A naval engagement between French and Spaniards in Falmouth harbour about
    1537   4

Bad animus of foreign powers against England at the same period   4

In 1537-9 (29-31, Hen. VIII) batteries and blockhouses were erected to protect
    Falmouth and other harbours...   4

In 1538, the oldest existing fortification of Pendennis (the block house) was erected   4

In 1539, the castle was ordered to be erected   4

Between 1542 and 1544, it was begun and finished   4

The tradition of King Hen. VIII's visit   5

Description of the castle and fortifications ... ...   5—6

Leland's Latin verse, and an English verse translation of it   7

Cannon and ammunition in the 16th century ... ...   7—8

CHAPTER II.

The site was held of the Killigrew family by the Crown, till 1795 ... ...   9—10

John Killigrew, captain or governor, 1544   10

    His death, 1567. Inscription in Budock Church   10

Sir John Killigrew, captain, 1567   10

    In 1569, he is described as captain of Falmouth, alias Pendennis castle ...   10

    He stays French vessels in 1570...   11

    The Earl of Bedford's account of the castle, 1574   11

    Sir J. Killigrew's death, 1584. Inscription at Budock   11

John Killigrew, captain, 1584   11

    He is not named in the list of captains by any Cornish historian   11

    Authority given to him to muster certain parishes for defence of the castle,
      1585   11

The Spanish "Floating Babel," 1588 ... ...11—12

"Barycades" to be constructed, 1593 12

Baskerville's letter relative thereto, and to the state of the ports in Cornwall, 1593, and 1595 ... ...13—14

John Killigrew's petition as to repairing and fortifying the castle, and for its supply with men, guns, &c. 10 men are already allowed to the castle. He requires 60 men, and 7 guns, &c. Makes a liberal offer, 1595 ... 15

His further petition, 1596 ... ...15—16

The captain's fees, 10s. per diem, 1596 16

Sir Francis Godolphin's estimate of the castle, 1597 16

Sir Nicholas Parker, captain 1597 16

He is empowered to exercise the charge of captain by deputy in case of necessity, 1598 ... ...16—17

Nicholas Burton his deputy 17

Sir N. Parker's account of the fortifying which is in progress. His complaint that he has only one piece of serviceable ordnance, 1598 17

The builder's account, 1598 17

Norden's account ... ...17—18

50 men allowed to the fort. Their wages 8d a day, 1598 18

Ordnance sent to the fort, June 1599 18

Complaint of Sir N. Parker, that he has received but 4 pieces for the front of the fort, which requires 12: and that ordnance in St. Mawes castle ought to be transfered to Pendennis, Aug. 1599 18

He has 45 men " and not one officer," Aug. 1599 18

Hals's account of the fortifying, munifying, and garrisoning... 18

Carew's statement of the garrison, 1602 19

Carew's eulogy of Sir N. Parker 19

Sir N. Parker's intimacy with Lady Jane Killigrew ... ...19—20

The Mayor's cup 20

Sir N. Parker's death, 1603. Inscription at Budock 21

John Parker, captain or keeper, 1603 21

He is not named in the list of captains by any Cornish historian 21

Sir John Parker, captain or keeper, 1607 21

He is not named in the list of captains by any Cornish historian 21

Sir Nicholas Hals or Halse said to have been governor in 1613 21

Probably he was lieutenant-governor 21

Sir N. Hals favours the project of building a new town (afterwards called Falmouth), at Smithike, representing how it would be advantageous to the castle of Pendennis, 1613 22

Sir Robert Killigrew, captain, 1614 22

He is not named in the list of captains by any Cornish historian 22

Distress of the soldiers of Pendennis castle, who have been without pay for 20 months. Their petition, 1625 ... ...22—23

Another petition of the distressed soldiers (50 men) 1625 23

Capt. John Bonython's complaint of the unprovided state of the castle, in two letters to Sec. Conway, 1626 23

Capt. John Bonython (and not Sir N. Hals) is deputy captain of Pendennis castle in 1626 23

The statements of Hals and Tonkin 23

Sir R. Killigrew's petition for a supply for the castle and alterations in the fortifications; and for pay for the garrison of 50 men, who have been all but starving, 1626 24

Sir John Killigrew's attempt to get Bonython removed from the deputy captainship, April and May, 1626 24

Bonython's further letters to Sec. Conway, Oct. & Nov. 1626 24

Sir R. Killigrew's further petition, 1627 24

Warrant to add 50 more men for defence of the castle, 1627 25

Commencement of the repairs and alterations of the fortifications, 1627 ... 25

It is conjectured that the distressed soldiers received their pay at about this time 25

The same Sir Robert Killigrew, jointly with his son, Sir William Killigrew, captain, 1628 25

They are not named in the list of captains by any Cornish historian 25

The grant to them of the captainship, with fees for them, and the garrison of 100 soldiers, and 40*l.* per ann. for reparation of the fort 25

John Tresahar, lieutenant-governor, in 1628, complains that the lieutenant at St. Mawes summons captains of ships to that castle ... .25—26

Strength of the garrison at a general muster 26

Sir W. Killigrew's complaint, that for the last 2 years ships have been stayed and questioned at St. Mawes castle, and this had been accustomed to be done at Pendennis castle only, 1630 26

After both sides have been heard, it is ordered, that Pendennis is to call to account ships which anchor on the west side, and St. Mawes, those which anchor on the east side, of the Black Rock, 1631 26

Sir W. Killigrew's petition to the king for that order to be stayed, 1631 26

The king, purposing to hear the differences himself, directs the order to be stayed in the meantime, 1631 ... ...26—27

Reduction of the garrison from 100 to 50 men, 1632 27

Sir R. Killigrew's protestation as this, 1632 27

Lord Arundel of Wardour's representation of the ill repair and the importance of the castle, 1634 27

Death of Sir Robert Killigrew, Nov. 1633... 27

Sir William Killigrew alone, captain, 1633 27

Surrender of the captainship by Sir W. Killigrew, April, 1635 27

CHAPTER III.

Sir Nicholas Slanning, governor, 1635   28

    John Tresahar, lieutenant-governor   28

    The king instructs Sir N. Slanning to take men and cannon from Pendennis
      on a secret expedition to Cumberland, 1639   28

    Commencement of the civil war, 1612   ... ...28—29

    Its nature   29

    Petition of Cornwall for repair of the castle ... ...29—30

    Sir N. Slanning slain at the battle of Bristol, 1643   30

Col. John Arundel, governor, 1643   30

    "John for the King."   "Old Tilbury"   30

    Col. Tremayne, or Richard Arundel, lieut.-governor   ... ...30—31

    The king's letter to Sir W. Killigrew, the former governor, promising for
      Col. Arundel's son, Richard, the reversion of the government after his
      father. 1643, Jan   31

    Col Arundel harbours Queen Henrietta Maria in Pendennis castle about the
      4th July, 1644   31

    Her flight thence .. ..31—32

    Powder supplied from the castle for the battle of Broadoak, 1644   32

    Duke of Hamilton a prisoner in the castle, 1644-5 ... ...32—33

    Sir E. Hyde (Lord Clarendon) sent to the castle to have the frigate there in
      readiness for the prince, 1645, Aug.   33

    Lord Norwich sues for the governorship, 1645, Oct.   33

    Prince Charles directs the castle to be prepared for his abode there in the
      winter, 1645, Oct.   33

    He orders an addition to the garrison, 1645, Nov.   34

    The removal of the Duke of Hamilton from the castle, 1645, Nov.   34

    The prince is troubled by the governor being misinformed that the prince
      intends to displace him, in favour of Lord Hopton, 1645, Nov.   34

    Col. Pickeringe is by Cromwell desired to be honourably interred, according
      to one authority, in Pendennis, 1645, Dec.   But this must be an error ...   35

    Pendennis is declared to be victualled for a year, 1646, Jan.   35

    Prince Charles repairs thither, about 16 Feb., 1646   36

    He hears of a design to seize his person, and his very servants are suspected   36

    "The king's room"   36

    He proposes to erect a chapel in the castle, 1646, Feb.   36

    He embarks from Pendennis, 2 Mar., 1646   37

    A contemporary newspaper account   37

    Lord Hopton sends his infantry and some ammunition to Pendennis and St.
      Michael's Mount, 1646, Mar.   37

The expectation that the castle will shortly surrender, 11 Mar., 1646 38

120 musqueteers, armed, come out of Pendennis, and yield themselves to Sir Thos. Fairfax, 14 Mar., 1646 38

Col. Arundel expects the coming of the parliament forces to Arwenack house, and succeeds in burning great part of it before their arrival, 16 Mar., 1646 ... ...38—39

Two regiments are quartered there and in Pennycomequicke, for the blocking up of the castle, 17 Mar., 1646 39

The expectation that the castle will soon be 'tractable,' 17 Mar. 39

The use of St. Mawes and Dennis castles, whose surrender was about the 16th and 18th March, in the operations against Pendennis ("T. M.'s" letter ... ...39—40

The royalist man of war protecting Pendennis on the 17th Mar. ("T. M.'s" letter) 40

The strength of the castle, as reported by one of the enemy, and his judgment as to how it may be reduced ("T. M.'s" letter) 41

A royalist frigate fought and taken in Falmouth harbour, 18 Mar., ("T. M.'s" letter, and a newspaper account) 41

Sir Thos. Fairfax's summons to the governor to surrender, 18 Mar. 42

Col. Arundel's reply, 18 Mar. 42

The investment by land and sea. The five months' siege 43

Newspaper judgment on the 23rd Mar. 43

Fortifications to be raised on the isthmus to block up Pendennis by land, 24 Mar. 43

An ambush, 26 Mar. 44

Pendennis "almost lined about" 28 Mar. 44

Lords Hopton and Capel embark from Pendennis, 11 April 44

Letter from the council of war at Pendennis to the prince, informing him of their state, and praying assistance. Provisions from Ireland for the 1500 in Pendennis hoped for. 11 April 44

The line nearly perfected for blocking up the castle, 15 April 44

Description of the entrenchments of the blockading forces 45

Description of the redoubt and works on the part of the defenders 45

Col. Hammond's summons to the governor to surrender, 17 April 45

Col. Arundel's reply, 17 April 45

He expects 800 more will besiege them, 19 April 45

The castle supposed to be on treaty for surrender, 19 April, (Col. Fortescue) 45

Its "ambitious glory" 27 April 46

Capt. Batten's summons to the castle to surrender, 30 April 46

Curious verses made in the castle, likening it to Penelope, her suitors being Fairfax, Hammond, Fortescue, and Batten, but her husband the King. May ... ...47—48

Directions for relief of the castle, 21 May   48

Col. Tremayne's escape   48

A ship with relief for the castle captured, 12 June   49

Those in the castle supposed to 'droop' in consequence, 15 June   49

Letter from the castle to the prince, saying they must, if not relieved, surrender in 3 weeks, 27 June   49

Soldiers 'run out' of the castle daily, and say the same thing, 30 June ...   49

Hopes of the enemy, 30 June   49

A sally by boats for fetching in relief, about 25 July   49

Ships with relief stayed by contrary winds, about 15 July   50

News sent by a shallop to the prince, about 26 July   50

Officers reject overtures made to them to quit the castle for the service of the king of Spain   50

Two hundred "great shot" fired from the castle in three days   50

Two shallops, in spite of Capt. Batten, bring relief to the castle, but the relief little, and the governor writes to Col. Fortescue, and takes two days time to consider whether he will treat, 2 Aug.   50

Order for killing horses for provisions for the garrison   51

The governor begins to treat, 10 Aug.   51

He breaks off, 12 Aug.   52

The resolve to blow up the castle, and fall upon the enemy, if honourable terms should be refused   52

The governor again begins to treat, 14 Aug.   52

Chief articles agreed, 15 Aug.   52

Articles all agreed, 16 Aug.   52

The articles   53-4-5-6-7

The marching out of Pendennis. The ordnance, &c. The officers. The sick. The women and children. The plot. (Capt. Batten's account) ...   57—8

What vessels, &c., were surrendered   58

Haslock's letter as to the plot, the surrender, and the provisions in the castle   58

The number and quality of the garrison   59

Parliament has letters as to the surrender, 21 Aug.   59

Lord Clarendon's eulogy ... ...59—60

That of Hals ... ...60—61

The house of commons nominates and approves of Col. Fortescue to be governor, 25 Aug.   61

The house orders payment of £60 to the messengers who brought the news of the surrender, 25 Aug.   61

A day of public thanksgiving ordered, 25 and 28 Aug.   61

Col. Richard Fortescue, governor, 1647   62

The house of commons allows Col. Fortescue to be governor, 12 Mar., 1647 ... 62

Sir Hardres Waller, governor, 1648 62

The house of commons orders the castle to be delivered up to Sir Hardres
Waller, and the lords agree, 17 April, 1648 63

Henry Flamank, his chaplain. A memorial of him... 63

Shrubsall lieut -governor 63

Alleged destruction by him of a ruined college... 64

Alleged injury of the loggan stone, &c., by soldiers from the castle 64

A fight, close to the castle, between Lord Hopton, upon his landing to
obtain provision, and the parliament forces, April, 1649 64

The house of commons considers about confirming the articles of surrender,
28 Mar., 1650 65

The house orders each of the four foot companies at the castle, to be completed to the number of 60. 10 May, 1650... 65

William Prynne a prisoner in the castle, 1652 65

His account of it 65

Character of Sir Hardres Waller... 65

Capt. John Fox, governor, 1658 66

Robert Roberts, lieut.-governor, 6 Aug., 1658 66

Lyson's account of the governorship 66

A letter from the governor is read in the house of commons, and referred to
the council of state 66

Col. Anthony Rowse, governor, 1659 66

The house of commons approves of him to be governor, 13 Feb., 1659 ... 66

He is not named by Cornish historians in the list of governors of Pendennis 66

The notice (presumably) of him by Hals, and its inaccuracies 67

CHAPTER IV.

Sir Peter Killigrew, governor, 1660 68

His interest in the site of the castle 68

The town at Smithicke named 'Falmouth,' 1660, and made a corporate
town, with a saving of the rights of Sir P. Killigrew, 1661 69

Five foot companies to be continued in the castle, under command of Col.
Richard Arundel, 1660 ? 69

Reduction of two of the five companies ordered, Jan. 1661 69

Probably Col. Rich. Arundel was deputy governor... 69

Petition of Lionel Gatford, D.D., late chaplain of the castle, Aug. 1661 ... 69

Warrant for Col. Harvey to be sent prisoner to the castle, Oct. 1661 69

A petition of one who served the king while he was at the castle, 1662 ... 69

Col Richard, afterwards Richard Lord Arundel, governor, 1662 70

Warrant to pay him £2000 for payment of the garrison, July, 1662 70

£377 10s. 8d. monthly, to be the pay of the three companies in the garrison
and their officers, Aug. 1662 70

Col. Legg, lieut.-governor, 1663   70

£1143 to be paid him for ammunition and provision for the castle, 1663 ...   70

Sir Nicholas Slanning to have the office of governor in reversion after Col.
Arundel, 1664   70

47 pieces of supernumerary ordnance unmounted, remaining in the castle,
to be sent to the tower, 1664   70

Parish of Falmouth formed. Pendennis retained as a (detached) portion of
Budock parish, 1664   70

The governor, Col. Richard, is created Lord Arundel, 1665   71

He is startled by a proposition to send 100 men, officered, to Plymouth, his
garrison being only 200, Nov. 1665   71

John Wildman to be imprisoned in the castle, 1666...   71

The works to be repaired and fortified, the garrison to be victualled for 2
months, and the allotted number of soldiers to be filled up, there being
apprehension of invasion, 1666   71

A Mr. Desborough imprisoned 3 months in the castle, by mistake for Major
General Desborough, 1666   72

Sir John Stevens probably lieut.-governor in 1666   72

The fire of London. Oaths of allegiance and supremacy to be taken by the
garrison. Only one, a Roman Catholic, refused Dec. 1666 ... ...72—73

The governor is to set John Wildman at liberty, Oct. 1667   73

The war with Holland being at an end. the soldiers in the castle, except 60,
are disbanded, Oct. 1667   73

John Lord Arundel, governor, 1667   73

Lyson's account of the governorship from 1660 to the Earl of Bath's time   73

Hals' account of the governorship from 1647 to the Earl of Bath's time ...73—74

John Grenville Earl of Bath, governor, about 1670   74

Anne Pomeroy's petition, 1671   74

Sir Peter Killigrew's violent taking of £201 from the king's collector, for
repair of the castle ; and confinement of the collector in the castle, 1689 ..   75

John Waddon, deputy governor   75

The earl's negotiations for delivering up the castle to the prince of Orange;
the earl to remain governor, 1689   75

Richard Trevanion, governor, 1697   75

Hals says he was governor   75

The castle struck by lightning, 1717   75

Fees of the governor (£182 15s.), of the lieut-governor (£73), and of the
gunners. 1719 (?)   76

Lieut-Colonel Arthur Owen, governor, about 1735   76

Lieut-Col. Richard Bowles, lieut-governor, from 1758 to 1769   76

Col. William Fawcett, lieut-governor, from 1769   76

The governor's death, 1774   76

Lieut-Colonel Charles Beauclerk, governor, 1774 76
    Col. Fawcett still lieut-governor 76
    The governor's death, 1775 76
Lieut-General Robert Robinson, governor, 1775 76
    Grose names him as governor 76
    Col Fawcett still lieut-governor till about 1776 76
    Major Newington Pool, lieut-governor, from 1776 76
    The fortress repaired, about 1780... 76
    Fees of governor and lieut-governor in 1787 76
    The governor's death, 1793 76
General Felix Buckley, governor, 1793... 76
    Lyson and Drew name him as governor 76
    Major Pool still lieut-governor 76
    Pendennis lands purchased by the crown, 1795 77
    Crab Quay Battery and Half Moon Battery added, about 1795 77
    Major Pool resigned the lieut.-governorship, 1797 77
    Capt. Philip Melvill, lieut-governor, from 1797 77
    Little dwellings and gardens made by the soldiers on the south west of the
        castle, encouraged by Capt. Melvill 77
    French prisoners in the castle, an object of his care... 77
    A memorial of him, by Drew 77
    His death, 1811. Inscription in Falmouth Church... 78
    Capt. James Considine, lieut-governor, 1811—1814 78
    Lieut-Col. William Fenwick, lieut-governor, from 1814 78
    The governor's death, 1823 78
General Sir M. Hunter, governor, 1823 78
    Lieut-Col. Fenwick, still lieut-governor, till 1832 78
    The governor's appointment to the governorship of Stirling castle, 1832 ... 78
General Paul Anderson, governor, 1832 78
    Brevet Lieut-Col. Loftus Gray, lieut-governor, from 1832 till his death, 1835 78
    The office thereupon abolished 78
    The governor appointed colonel of the 78th Reg. of foot, 1837 78
    The office of governer thereupon abolished 78
The modern system 78

ST. MAWES CASTLE.
CHAPTER I.

Origin of name. Different derivations 79
Variations upon the name 79
Connection of the name with that of St. Malo 80

The saint's residence at both places in the 6th century 80

Date of building, 1542, or a little earlier 81

Its cost 5000*l*. 81

Inscriptions ... ...81—82

Description of the building 82

The tradition of King Hen. VIII's visit 83

Leland's verse... 7

Chapter II.

Michael Vyvyan, captain, keeper, or governor, 1544 84

    Hals was misinformed about Sir R. Greice being the first captain 84

    The site and the government of the castle given to Michael Vyvyan, by
    King Henry VIII 84

    The castle strengthened and enlarged with two barbacans, about 1550 ... 85

    Death of Michael Vyvyan, 1561 85

Hannibal Vyvyan, captain or keeper, 1651 85

    An estimate made of ordnance for the castle, 1577 85

    Hannibal Vyvyan insists upon having a better supply of ordnance, &c.,
    viz.: a whole culverin, 4 demi-culverins, 3 sakers, &c., 1595 85

    His fees, 10s. per diem, 1596 85

    Carew's statement of the garrison, 1602 85

    His notice of 'Master Vivian,' 1602 85

Sir Francis Vyvyan, captain, 1603 85

    The grant to him of the office 86

    The expense of repairing the castle estimated by Sir Wm. Godolphin
    and others, 1609 86

    Commissioners recommend for 700*l*. to be granted for fortification of the
    castle; and 10 pieces of ordnance to be allowed to it, 1623 86

    Their description of the castle, as strong, &c., but overtopped with high
    ground, 1623 86

    A warrant given to Sir Francis for 253*l*. for repairs and provisions, 1628... 86

    Hannibal Bonithon, lieutenant-governor in 1630 86

    Sir Wm. Killigrew, captain of Pendennis castle, complains of Bonithon's
    staying and questioning ships at St. Mawes, 1630 86

    The certificate of the Trinity House as to the consequence or use of the
    castle, 1631 86

    Certificates of the borough of St. Mawes, &c., that the staying and
    questioning of ships at the castle, has been long accustomed, 1631 ... 86

    Bonithon's petition to the Admiralty, setting forth the chief points
    deserving consideration, touching the difference between the castles,
    Feb. 1631 87-8-9-90

After the Admiralty have heard both sides, they order, that Pendennis is to call to account ships which anchor on the west side, and St. Mawes those which anchor on the east side, of the Black Rock. May, 1631 ...   90

Sir Wm. Killigrew, of Pendennis, petitions for that order to be stayed, July, 1631   90

The king will hear the differences himself, and directs the execution of the order to be stayed in the meantime, July, 1631   90

The Star Chamber sentences Sir Francis Vyvyan to be committed to the Fleet, to pay a fine of 2000*l.*, and to be removed from his office of captain of St. Mawes, declaring him to have practised certain deceptions in reference to his office, Nov. 1632   90

His fine of 2000*l.* is respited, Feb. 1633   91

CHAPTER III.

Sir Robert le Grys, captain, 1632...   92

Charges made against him as captain, which he answers, April, 1633   ...   92

He appoints John Stanbury lieutenant of the castle, 1634   92

The Admiralty deprive him, and appoint Capt. Bonithon to be continued in the office, 1634   92

Commissioners for survey of the castle, estimate the cost of necessary repairs at 534*l.* Aug. 1634   92

There were a master gunner and 12 soldiers in the castle, Aug. 1634   ...   93

Fees for the porter and gunner 12d., and every soldier 8d. per diem   ...   93

Thomas Howard, Earl of Arundel and Surrey, captain, 1635   93

Curious terms of the grant to him   93

He is not named as governor by Cornish historians   93

Hannibal Bonithon still lieutenant of the castle, 1635...   93

A report on the castle. Fees for the captain, 3s., the lieutenant, 18d., and soldiers, 8d. per diem, 1836   93

Depositions charging Bonithon with embezzlement, disaffection to the king's cause, &c., Sept. 1645...   94

Major Hannibal Bonithon's surrender of the castle to Sir Thos. Fairfax, Mar. 1646   94

His relation that the reputation of the treaty of Tressilian Bridge had produced a surrender of the castle, wherein were found 13 guns, &c...   95

Another contemporaneous account. Two great brass cannon found in the castle   95

Col. Arundel's invitation to Major Bonithon   95

Lieutenant-Colonel Kekewich, captain, 1646   96

His appointment by the parliament   96

Hals's error as to the governorship, &c.   96

Sir Richard Vyvyan, captain, 1660   97

His petition for a few more soldiers, there being only 1 gunner, and 12 soldiers, 1660   97

Establishment of the garrison. Fees for governor, 8s., and deputy-governor, 8s., and 200 soldiers each 8d. per diem, &c., &c., 1664 ... 97

89*l.* allowed for repairs, 1664 98

Warrant for a grant to Viel Vivian, in reversion after Sir Richard, of the office of captain, 1665 98

Death of Sir Richard, Oct. 1665 98

Sir Vyel Vyvyan, captain, 1665 98

Account of the sale by him of the castle lands, to John Earl of Bath ... 98

Death of Sir Vyel, 1696 98

Sir Joseph Tredenham, captain, 1696 99

The transfer to him of the castle lands, 1696... 99

Mr. Boscawen, his deputy 99

Sir Joseph displaced in 1697 99

The Right Honourable Hugh Boscawen, afterwards Viscount Falmouth, captain, 1697 99

Sir Joseph Tredenham prayed payment of the clearings due to himself, his late deputy, and gunners, and payment was to be made, 1698 ... 99

How the castle was armed. Fees of captain, deputy and gunners (Hals' account), 1719 99

The captain made Viscount Falmouth, 1720 99

His death, 1734 100

Major de Roen, captain, 1734 100

Adjutant General Scipio Duroure, captain, about 1740 100

His death, 1745. Inscription in Westminster Abbey 100

Lieutenant General Alexander Duroure, captain, 1745 100

His death, 1765. Inscription in Westminster Abbey 100

Lieutenant General Sir R. Pigot, Bart., captain, 1765 100

His death, 1796 100

Colonel Edward Morrison, captain, 1796 100

His appointment to be governor of Chester, 1796 100

Field Marshall Sir George Nugent, Bart., captain, 1796 100

Who were the owners of the castle lands in 1814 101

Major Aloes, deputy governor, 1812—1815 101

Lieut.-Colonel Graham, deputy governor, 1815—1828 101

Major General Sir Alexander Cameron, deputy governor, 1828—1842 ... 101

The office abolished, 1842 101

Death of the captain, 1849 101

The office abolished, 1849 101

The modern system 101

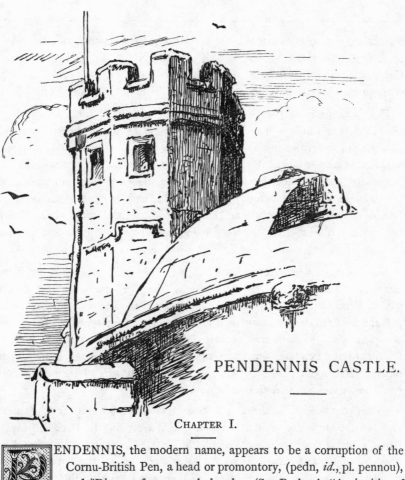

PENDENNIS CASTLE.

CHAPTER I.

PENDENNIS, the modern name, appears to be a corruption of the Cornu-British Pen, a head or promontory, (pedn, *id.*, pl. pennou), and *Dinas, a fortress or bulwark. (See Borlase's "Antiquities of Cornwall.") Dr. William Pryce, 1790, in his "Archæologia Cornu-Britannia" gives the same derivation. The account given by Hals is somewhat different. He says (p. 129), "the Compound Name *Pen-den-is* Castle,

---

* Across the bay at the mouth of the Helford river at Condorah, in the parish of St. Anthony (Meneague) is a fortified headland called the little Dinas or Dinas Vean. "This little Dinas has several modern fortifications on its eastern point (erected in the Great Rebellion); but nearer to Condorah it has an old Vallum stretching from sea to sea, which is the remainder of a very ancient fortification, and in all likelihood, Roman."— Borlase's Antiquities, p. 290.

it's British, and signifies that it is the *head* or *chief Man's Castle*, viz., the King or Earl of *Cornwal*'s. Otherwise, if the true Name thereof be *Pen-dun-es* Castle, it signifies that it is the *head* or *chief Fort* or Fortress *Castle.*" There is also a Pendinas near St. Ives, and probably there are others in Cornwall.

The promontory of Pendennis is almost an island. Leland says (vol. 3, fol. 10). "It is a Mile in Cumpace by the Cumpace and is almost environid with the Se. and where it is not, the Ground is so low, and the Cut to be made so litle that it were insulatid." And again (fol. 5), "*Pendinas* almost an isle." Norden (p. 50), describes it as "a peninsula lying poyntinge into the sea at ye mouth of Falmouth Haven;" and adds, "It hath bene, as it seemeth, an Ilande; in the whole prouince no Iland comparable; the forme whereof may be thus described:" And then upon the same page he gives us a ground plan of "Pendenis *Ilande,*' saying, "It is aboue 1½ myle in circuit."

There is no evidence to show at what period the noble promontory of Pendennis was first fortified, but at all events from the time when it was first named Pendennis or Pendinas, it, doubtless, was the site of a hill-fort, built, perhaps, by the Ibero-Aquitanian invaders in pre-historic times. That it was occupied by the Romans seems nearly certain. Borlase says (p. 291), "From the situation of Pendinas—more advantageously shap'd for defence, and guard of a noble Harbour (call'd by Ptolemy, *Cenionis Ostium;)* I should guess it could never escape the notice and use of the Romans."

In the year 806, A.D., the Danes came into Cornwall and brought a fleet there at the invitation of the Cornish. Still, according to Borlase (p. 44), "they winter'd not here in Britain, till the year 854, as is particularly taken notice of by the historians. It seems, it was their custom to return every year to their own country, either to carry off their spoil, to visit their wives and children, to recruit their forces, or to repair their ships, which could not be so well done, or so securely attended to, in a foreign, and enemy's country. This frequent sailing to and fro brought them acquainted with all the secure landing places on the coast, where, if the winds would not permit them to land in one place, they soon knew where, in some other adjacent creek, they might shelter their ships, and disbark their men with more safety and conveniency; if they could not securely put on shore a great number in one place, 'tis natural to imagine that they would divide into parties, and land as near one to the other as possible : this, the many landing places so very little distant from each other round the extremity of Cornwall (call'd the Land's End), do abundantly testify : as the Danes were so frequently obliged to land, and embark again, another thing occurs to every one who will consider their works, (for works are records and oftentimes the only remaining proofs and grounds of history) and 'tis this, that not caring easily to quit any land where they had once got footing, and yet knowing well enough to provide for a secure retreat to their ships on all events, they not only entrench'd themselves on the hills, but soon learn'd (so instructive is necessity) to intrench and fortify their landing-places."

At about this period, therefore, sometime in the 9th century, but according to Gilbert, A.D. 807, the promontory of Pendennis is believed to have been fortified, as Gilbert has it, by the Danes, with a triple intrenchment of turf, earth and stones, enclosing an area of 20 acres ; but, according to Polwhele, this triple entrenchment was Roman or British. And Hals says (p. 129), "This Castle of old consisted only of a treble Intrenchment of Turf, Earth and Stones, after the British or Roman manner, upon the Top of the highest Hill in those parts." Where this triple intrenchment may have been, there is no trace to shew. In all probability it would be across the narrow neck of ground where the Falmouth Hotel now stands, or between that and the docks.

No further fortification of Pendennis appears to have been attempted until the time of Henry VIII.*

In the year 1537—the fact is noted in Froude's history (vol. 3, p. 248)—"the harbours in general were poorly defended, and strange scenes occasionally took place in their waters." For an example the historian cites (pp. 248-9), a report by one John Arundel, of Trerice, to one Cromwell, of a spirited naval

---

* "This most provident Prince, having shaken off the more than servile yoke of Popish tyrannie, and espying that the Emperor was offended for his divorce from Queen Katherine, his aunt, and thereto under-standing that the French King had coupled the Dauphin his son with the Pope's niece, and married his daughter to the King of Scots (1537), he determined to stand upon his own defense, and therefore with no small speed, and like charges, he builded certain blokehouses, castles, and platforms upon divers frontiers of the Realme."—*(Grafton,* as cited in the 26th Ann. Rep. Roy. Inst. of Corn., p. 28)

"The same time the King caused all the hauens to be fensed with bulworks and blockehouses, and riding to Douer he took order to haue bulworks made alongst the sea coasts."—*Holinshed,* vol. III, p. 946, anno 1539.

engagement between French and Spaniards in Falmouth Harbour. At the conclusion of the report, Arundel says, "My lord, I and all the country will desire the King's Grace that we may have blockhouses made upon our haven." The historian adds (pp. 254.5) : "The animus of foreign powers was evidently as bad as possible. Subjects shared the feelings of their rulers. The Pope might succeed, and most likely would succeed at last, in reconciling France and Spain ; and experience proved that England lay formidably open to attack. It was no longer safe to trust wholly to the extemporized militia. The introduction of artillery was converting war into a science ; and the recent proofs of the unprotected condition of the harbours should not be allowed to pass without leaving their lesson. Commissions were issued for a survey of the whole eastern and southern coasts. The most efficient gentlemen in the counties which touched the sea were requested to send up reports of the points where invading armies could be most easily landed, with such plans as occurred to them for the best means of throwing up defences. The plans were submitted to engineers in London ; and in two years (1537-1539) every exposed spot upon the coast was guarded by an earthwork, or a fort or block-house. Batteries were erected to protect the harbours at St. Michael's Mount, Falmouth, Fowey, Plymouth, Dartmouth, Torbay, Portland, Calshot, Cowes and Portsmouth. Castles were built at Dover, Deal, Sandwich, and along both shores of the Thames."

In the year 1538 then, we may conclude, was erected the oldest existing fortification of Pendennis, viz., the small block-house close to the water's edge near the present rifle range. In the same year the monasteries were suppressed.

It would appear, (see 26th Annual Report of the Royal Institution of Cornwall, p. 28), according to the calculation of Sir Charles Lemon, Bart. (M.P., President Royal Institution of Cornwall in 1844), that the order for the erection of Pendennis castle was given in the year 1539, and that the building of it was "begun and finished between 1542 and 1544," when Leland, the author of the Itinerary, saw it. (Cf. *post.*) The castle may be considered, therefore, co-eval with the printing of the first authorized translation of the bible (Cranmer's). Carew (p. 362) tells us : " On the west side, at the very coming in, there riseth a hill, called Pendennis, where King Henry the Eighth, when he took order for fortyfying the seacoasts, caused a castle to be builded, with allowance of a petty garrison, and some small store of ordnance." Neither he, Leland, Camden, nor any other Cornish historian, gives any precise date.

The oldest part of the castle or citadel of Pendennis, is, therefore, at the present date not less than three hundred and thirty years old. It appears to have been built under the superintendence of a Mr. Treffry, of Fowey, who also built the other fortifications along the coast.

"It is said that the King [Henry VIII] came to view the situation of his two projected Castles of St. Mawes and Pendennis ; that he passed two nights at Tolvern, then a seat of the Arundells ; and that he crossed the river from thence to Feock, at a passage that has ever since gone by his name. There is not, however, any trace of this journey to be found in histories of the times, nor in any public document."—(Gilbert, vol. 2, p. 280). Gilbert, how-ever, (p. 280) speaks of the tradition as "universally believed in Cornwall."

The original building, with the exception of the exterior gate and guard-house, must remain in much the same state as when first erected ; at all events we can well judge of what it was originally. What alterations have been made in it, have certainly not added to its state or beauty, however they may have added to its security.

The great tower is circular, 35 feet in height, and 56 feet in exterior diameter, with granite walls, 11 feet thick, pierced with circular and arched embrasures to casements, in three tiers for artillery. The summit is also provided with embrasures for artillery, the whole surmounted on the north side, with a small look-out turret embattled for ornament ; this was probably surmounted with a cupola, but in place of a cupola there is now only a small flagstaff.

To the north from this tower projects a wing or block, which is of lower elevation ; this is embattled and is of two stories. In this are the state apartments, and it has a highly ornamented gateway approached by a draw-bridge. The whole is encircled with a parapet wall, whose trace is a quindecagon, with embrasures for cannon, outside which again are a circular ditch and a slight glacis. A guard-room protects the outer end of the drawbridge.

The rougher portion of the solid masonry is composed of granite from quarries at Mabe and elsewhere in the neighbourhood; but the finer decorated portions of the stonework are wrought in the famous Polruddon or Pentowan stone, from the neighbourhood of St. Austell. Leland mentions "a fair quarre of whit free stone on the shore rokks betwixt St. Pentowan and Blak-hed, whereof sum be usid in the inward parts of St. Maure forteresse; and Pendinas castelle is of the same stone except the wallinge." Carew mentions this stone in the parish of St. Austell as somewhat resembling grey marble; and Norden calls it " the best free stone that Cornwall yealdeth, and the most of the churches and towres thereabout were buylded of them." (See Hitchins and Drew, vol. 2, p. 352).

The following is taken from Hitchins and Drew's History, published in 1824. "This celebrated fortress stands on the summit of a verdant hill, gently sloping towards the isthmus which connects it with the mainland, but descending with more abruptness towards the sea.......This fortress, which is built of Cornish granite, is proudly exalted on an elevation upwards of 300 feet from the sea, from which the whole entrance of the harbour is commanded. [In the Parochial History of Cornwall, published by Lake, vol. 1, p. 155, the elevation above the sea at low water is said to be 198 feet]. The fortifications, which are of an irregular shape, include an area of between three and four acres. On the north or land side, it is defended by four cavaliers; and the traces of a horn and crown work constructed during the civil war, are at a short distance. The banks of the ditch and citadel still remain; the situation of which was admirably calculated to check the progress of an enemy over the isthmus. On the east, near the water's edge, is a battery of five guns called Crab Quay; and on the hill above is a half-moon battery. Within the works are convenient barracks for troops, magazines and storehouses." (Vol. 2, pp. 255-6).

Leland, in his *Cygnea Cantio*, (lines 548-552), writes thus of the castles of Pendennis and St. Mawes :—

> Pendinas tenet asperi cacumen
> Celsum montis, et intonat frequenter.
> Mauditi quoque subsidet rotundum
> Castrum, et fulminat impetu furenti,
> Portus ostia quà patent Falensis.

An English verse translation of these lines is given in Camden's Britannia, by Gibson (vol. 1, p. 150). It is the following :—

> High on a craggy rock Pendennis stands,
> And with its thunder all the port commands ;
> While strong St. Maudit's answers it below,
> Where Falmouth's sands the spacious harbour show.

In King George the Third's collection at the British Museum, there is an excellent drawing of Pendennis castle, north east view, by Buck, 1734.

With what description of cannon the castle was defended in the earliest period after its erection, it is impossible to say, but it seems highly probable that there were guns in it, rudely formed of iron bars welded together, and bound by hoops of the same metal, and that they threw stone shot. Cast iron cannon were first made in England about 1545, and brass cannon seven or eight years previously : stone shot were fired from the wrought-iron guns, and iron shot from the cast-iron and from the brass guns. (See 26th Ann. Rep. Roy. Inst. of Corn., p. 31).

At about the date of the erection of Pendennis castle, cannon of iron and bronze, under the names of guns, bombards, canon, and scloppi or schioppi, and bound down to large heavy wooden beds or craddils, were employed in sieges, both for attack and defence. Projectiles of lead, stone, iron, and in Italy even bronze were thrown by them, also arrows, and a species of carcass composition called Greek fire.

But it appears, from the length of time during which sieges lasted, that the art of opening a practicable breach by means of cannon, had not yet been mastered. Indeed, it is very doubtful whether with such powders as were used, sufficient force could have been obtained for that purpose. Powder was still a comparatively feeble agent ; the ingredients, pounded by hand in a mortar, were themselves but imperfectly purified, the gas must have passed very slowly through the mixture, and an immense quantity of the charge must have been blown out without being ignited. To prevent excessive windage the leaden shot were driven forcibly home into the bore of the piece by means of a mallét and drift, and the soft nature of the metal allowed them to completely fill the bore. With iron and stone shot, fired from the large guns, no drift was used, but the shot was inserted from the muzzle, and the powder by a scoop from the breech, which was then closed by a wooden tompion. The hot iron was used to fire the charge through a vent, which was often covered to keep the powder dry. But, rough as these appliances were, we must not despise too much the cannon of those days. They were suited to the age, and we have record of one shot killing twenty-two men.

A stone shot of 12½ lbs. weight and 20 inches in circumference, was dredged up in Falmouth harbour in 1844, and Sir Charles Lemon conjectures, that it was fired, towards the end of the reign of Elizabeth, from Pendennis, from a piece called a basilisk, at a Spanish privateer in chase of a merchant ship, and was one of the last stone shot ever fired in England. (See 26th Annual Report of the Royal Institution of Cornwall, p. 33.)

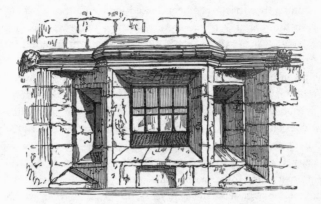

Chapter II.

HE SITE of Pendennis castle at the time of the building, and long afterwards, was held by the Crown of the Killigrew family, of Arwenack, at a small yearly rent and a fine.

John Leland, librarian and antiquary to King Henry VIII, visited Pendennis at about the time of the erection of Pendennis castle, and he, in his Itinerary (vol. 3, fol. 10), writes, " The very point of the haven mouth being an hille whereon the King hath buildid a castel is caullid Pendinant and longgith to Mr. Keligrewe." Tonkin, writing nearly two hundred years later, says, " The Killigrews are also Lords of the land whereon the Castle of Pendennis stands, and receive yearly out of the Exchequer for the same £13 6s. 8d." (And see Hals, p. 129.)

" Killigrew's the Lord both of the Fort and Town."

A petition to the Council, which is preserved amongst the State Papers (Dom. Ser. vol. 342, fol. 58), and the date of which is supposed to be 1636, sets forth that the hill contains about 60 acres, and is worth

£35 per annum, but that it has been leased for his majesty's use, by Sir John Killigrew, at the rent of £12 10s. And Martin Killigrew's MS. history of the Killigrews, written in 1737 or 1738, gives an account different in some particulars from the accounts of Hals and Tonkin. An abstract of this MS. history is given in the twelfth number of the Journal of the Royal Institution of Cornwall, for April, 1871, pp. 269-282, where it is stated (p. 269), that "the original is not known to exist." At p. 280 is found the following : " Martin Killigrew goes on to relate somewhat tediously, how Sir Peter [Killigrew (he was captain of the castle from 1660 to 1662)], after some years soliciting at the Treasury for justice to be done him as to Pendennis Castle—till then held on a long lease, at £2,000 fine and £12 10s. yearly rent—got the government to take a lease for 21 years, at £200 a year, without a fine, and retired to Ludlow in 1697." In 1795, the Pendennis lands were purchased from Sir John Wodehouse, the then representative of the Killigrew family (Lyson, vol. 3, p. xcvi), in fee, for the crown's use.

The first captain or governor of Pendennis castle, was John Killigrew, Esq., who was appointed by King Henry VIII, about the time when the building was completed, and two or three years before the King's death, probably in the year 1544. (See Journal Royal Institution of Cornwall, No. XII, p. 272). This John Killigrew remained captain through the reigns of Edward VI. and Mary, and until his death in the ninth year of Elizabeth. He was buried in the parish church of Budock, where (see Lake, vol. I, p. 150) a brass has the following inscription :—

" Here lyeth John Killigrew, Esqier, of Arwenack, and Lord of ye Manor of Killigrew, in Cornwall ; and Elizabeth Trewinnard, his wife. He was the first captaine of Pendennis Castle, made by King Henry the eight, so continued until the nynth of Queen Elizabeth, at which time God took him to his mercye, being the year of our Lord 1567. Sir John Killigrew, knight, his sone, succeeded him in ye same place by the gift of Queene Elizabeth."

Sir John Killigrew, son of the first captain, succeded his father both at Arwenack and at Pendennis in 1567. (Jour. Roy. Inst. Corn., XII, April, 1871, p. 272).

He appears not to have been created a knight before the year 1574. The State Papers contain an account of artillery and stores delivered to John Kylligrew, Esq., captain of Falmouth, alias Pendennis castle, dated 27th

March, 1569 (Dom. Ser. vol. 49, no. 74) ; and a letter from John Kylligrew to the Council, dated 30th July, 1570, in which he mentions, that he has stayed several French vessels in the harbour of Falmouth, but has given them hopes of a quick discharge (vol. 71, no. 69). And among the Landsdowne MSS. (18, art. 93), there is a letter from the Earl of Bedford to the Lord Treasurer, dated 3rd Aug. 1574, in which the Earl states, that he has been " over Cornwal, to view ye strength of y^t County," and that the castle in Mr. Killigrew's charge, is in very ill condition and unserviceable.

Sir John Killigrew remained captain of Pendennis castle until his death, in the year 1584. He was buried in the parish church of Budock, and a brass there (see Lake, vol. 1, p. 150) has the following inscription :—

" Here lyeth the bodies of Sir John Killigrewe, of Arwenack, in the Countye of Cornwall, knight, who departed this life the 5 day of March, Anno XXVI, Rne. of Eliz., and Dame Mary, his wife, daughter of Philip Wolverston, of Wolverston-Hall, in the countie of Suff :, esq. He was the second captain that commanded Pendennis Forte since the first erection thereof. He had issue by his saide wife 3 sonnes, viz., John, Thomas, and Symon ; and 2 daughters, Mary and Katherine. John, his sonne, married Dorothy, daughter of Thomas Monck, of Poderridge. in the county of Devon, Esq., by whom he had issue IX sonnes and 5 daughters, in whose memorie John Killigrewe, grand-sonne unto Sir John Killigrewe, hath of a pious mind erected this monument, An. D'm'i., 1617."

Sir John Killigrew was succeeded in the government of Pendennis castle by his eldest son, John Killigrew, in 1584. Not one of the historians of Cornwall names him in the list of captains. But there are preserved in the Record Office several State Papers, which are of considerable interest in connection with his captaincy. One supposed to be written by the Council to the Commissioners of Musters in 1585, contains an authority for John Killegrew, Esq., captain of Pendennis castle, to muster certain adjacent parishes, and to summon them when necessary for the defence of the castle. (Dom. Ser., vol. 185, no. 54).

" In the year 1588, when the Spanish floating Babel pretended the conquest of our island (which, like Joshua's army, they compassed, but, unlike him, could not, with their blasting threats, overthrow our walls), it pleased her Majesty, of her provident and gracious care, to furnish Cornwall with ordnance and ammunition, from her own store, as followeth,—Two Sacres, two Minions, two Faulcons, of cast iron, well mounted upon carriages with wheels shod with iron, and furnished with ladles, sponges, and rammers, with other necessaries.

Shot of iron for the said pieces of each sort, twenty." (Carew, p. 213). With regard to these pieces of ordnance, Sir Charles Lemon remarks (26th Ann. Rep. Roy. Inst. Corn., p. 27), "I do not think it at all probable that any of this artillery was sent to Pendennis—they appear to have been field guns, intended to be moved from place to place, and not for the regular defence of a castle; for the sacres carried only a five pound ball, the minions four pound, and faulcons, two pound." Sir Charles thinks that "the mention of *iron* shot seems to imply that the use of other shot had not so far passed out of recollection as to make it unnecessary to specify the sort of material with which the guns were supplied."—*(Ibid.)*

Five years later, in August 1593, an order had been taken with the deputy-lieutenants to "barycadee" all the ports in Cornwall; as appears, together with other interesting matter, in a paper published in the Journal of the Royal Institution of Cornwall, No. XIV., for April, 1873, contributed by Mr. Rowett, of Polperro, in which we read as follows :—

"The following letter, in the Cottonian Collection of Manuscripts, saved from the fire at Ashburnham House, October 23, 1731, and now in the British Museum (Cottonian MSS., Otho E, XI., fol. 230), shows the state of the ports in Cornwall in 1593-5.

"The portions burnt (indicated by italics) have been supplied by a careful study of the context.

"The "Barycades" alluded to, were, doubtless, hastily constructed fortifications on the coast.

"A map of the coasts of Devonshire and Cornwall, without date, but evidently made at the same time, and now in the British Museum, (Cottonian MSS., Aug : 1 : vol. I : 6), represents this plan of fortifications ; of which, Sir Thomas Baskerville says : "the placis where to sett those Barycades I have shewid them." It is labelled: "A plott of all the Coast of Cornwall and Devonshire, as they were to be fortyfied in 1588, against the landing of any Enemy ;" very neatly drawn on vellum, on two sheets, measuring together 5 ft. 2 in. × 2 ft. (Cott : Aug. I., 1. 6). This has been engraved by Pine, and was published with his plates of the tapestry hangings of the House of Lords, which represented the defeat of the Spanish Armada.—See also the " Report on the arrangements which were made for the internal defence of these king-doms, when Spain by its Armada projected the invasion and conquest of England ;" privately printed in 1798, by the late John Bruce, Esq., of the State Paper Office.

" *To the*
> Most honorab*le the Lords of her ma*^{ties}

> > *Most Honorable pryvy Counsell.*

May itt pleas your Lordshippe to be advertis*ed that accor*ding to your comandement I have bin in Corn*wall and* have vewid all the porte towns and crikes, bothe *on the south* and northe sea, and would have seen the s*outhern* cuntry perticulerly in their divisions, w^toutt dr*awing them* into one body/ iff the sisis* had nott bin so *very great and* the most parte of the gentillmen and cuntry*men had so* many defecks [as] I fynd in the porte towns, and fear *also* in the rest of the cuntry, for I asure your L*ordshipe* they have neyther† store of munysions nor good *arms* and for the most parte of the towns lytell or noe *arms are at* all left in them, The reason is this they being s*o guarded* cary their armes w^t them for their defence to the sea, *The* order taken w^t the deputie Lyftenants, for the better def*ence of* those placis is this ; first to Bary-cadee all those towns *as* strongly as may be, the placis wher to sett those Baryca*des* I have shewid them ; Then to take such order that nonn take any Arms to sea w^t hym, w^toutt leaving the preporcion he is charged w^t for the defence of his towne, and th*at* the mayor or other officers shall cause a revew wekly to be taken, and when any such defalt is fownd to punishe acordingly/.

Lykwise fynding greatt inconvenienc and *difficulti*es growe to the porte towns by reason of the ar*my which* is now held ther, wch is thatt the traynid Bands *are* composedid of the best menn of all the country, and *the*rfor taken outt of many placis so distant that some *of* them come 20 mills to their rande-vous, by wch means *our* best menn being drawene from the towns upon the cost, have left them to the spoyle of the enymy, therfore w^t the advise of

---

* In an accompanying note, Mr. Rowett says, the word " sisis" is intended for *sizes.*
† This word is written in substitution for the cancelled "*lytell.*"

deputies Lyftenant itt is thought for in som poynts to alter thatt course and to order itt in this sorte, that no Captain of the traynid Bands shall draw a mann from the porte towns or villagis next adjoÿnyng w^tin 2 or 3 mylles, butt all those having their randevòusis aparte and officers apoyntid in every village to comand them shall upon all alarams draw themselfs by the conduckt of the saÿd officers to the porte towne apoyntid for their gard, wher som gentillmann of worthe, thatt dwels next unto the saÿd porte is to take charg of them and of thatt place as of his garÿson, and he *is* by no means to w^t draw hymself outt of thatt place to the aÿd and assistance of any other towne, butt ther to abide at the place apoyntid to his charg/ the rest of the traynid and untraynid bands wch ar raysid outt of the inner parte of the cuntery ar to draw themselvs into divers heds or one as they shall see cause to second any town [that] shal be atemptid, this course is taken as most answerable to the nature of the atempt now mad·upon this coste, and will contÿnue till your Lordshypps further order, Lykwise the deputies Lyfftenants for the better *garding and* for the better ordering of the cunt*ry will continue to* make a generall review on in another deby*rtment dai*lÿe [to] se all the defecks suplÿed, the occasion of *which* is growen by favoring their pore neybours, *If you* shuld so thinke itt fitt itt were not amis to se*nd an exper*encid captaine to see thess things per-form*ed The menn* duthe verÿ much desir to have som captains sen*t to* them to lead them if the lÿke ocasions prey*vail. They* desi:id me in my letters to your Lordshipp to *say this* much unto you, as they will do lykwise in the*ir part.* so craving pardon for my so teadious *Letter* I humbley take my leave he who desirs to doe *your*

           Lordships all servis

             THO BASKERVILE

Plymouthe this 5 of August.

      The letter bears the following endorsements :

5 Aug : 1593.
       1595.
Sr Thomas Baskervyle
    to ye Consill pr^o
      Plymoth.

      To the most Honorable
      the Lords of her ma^{tis}
      most Honorable pryvÿ
         Counsell.

A petition of John Killigrew to the Council, the date of which has been supposed to be 1591, but I think, from comparison of the petition next mentioned, it must have been 1595, is preserved amongst the State Papers (Dom. Ser., vol. 240, No. 113), and is of considerable interest. In this petition he sets forth, that he, having charge of the castle, was sent for, with Sir Nicholas Parker and Paul Jaye, concerning the strengthening, and he has sent several petitions to their Lordships the last 6 or 7 years; that it was viewed 2 or 3 years past, by Sir Ferdinando Gorges, who thought that, by reason of the hill, the castle might be so fortified as to command the block-house and the whole hill, or as much as might be offensive to the castle, and that 1,400*l* or 1,500*l* would suffice, together with seven pieces of artillery, and some men, ammunition, &c. The petitioner offers to perform the work, so as to save Her Majesty the pay of 70 men, amounting to 700*l* or 800*l* yearly. He represents that 100 men are required in other instances for making new fortifications, while he demands but 60 in garrison; 10, he says, are already allowed to the castle, and 20 more are in pay; and this is the only expense he desires to charge Her Majesty with; he will himself maintain the other 30, his tenants offering their services, it being to their good, as while they are attending the service of the castle they are kept from all other county charges. He begs consideration of these offers; is no soldier, yet a true subject, with heart and mind to defend the place with his life; and, although the loss of life would be but little, he would lose with it a house not far from the castle, and the living appertaining to it, for if the enemy possessed the castle they would have that also; though it is of no great value, yet it is his whole commonwealth, and would be the overthrow of his posterity, who depend upon it. He does not desire to receive the money, but it may be left in such hands as their Lordships think fit; if the sum demanded do not finish the fortifications, he has 200*l* as rents of assize in Her Majesty's hands, which will be a sufficient pawn for finishing them as offered. The parishes adjoining the castle may send 400 fighting men into the castle, in less than three hours, which is as soon as any might be landed.

On the 6th Feb., 1596, he writes a letter from Pendennis castle to the Council. I pray you (he says), in this dangerous time, to consider for the fortifying, furnishing, and victualling of Pendennis castle ; better that 1,000 men should lose their lives than that the enemy should possess the place, which would cost many lives and much wealth to regain. Sir Henry Palmer knows its defects ; I have been twelve months a suitor about it, and have made a liberal offer, considering my beggarly estate, for its fortifying. (Dom. Ser., vol. 256, no. 40.)

From an account, dated 23 Mar., 1596, (St. Pa. Dom. Ser. vol. 261, no. 108), it appears that the yearly fee paid to John Killigrew, as captain of Pendennis castle, was £118 12s. 6d. ; that is 10s. per diem.

Sir Fras. Godolphin, in a letter to Secretary Cecil, dated 31st Dec. 1597, (St. Pa. Dom. Ser. vol. 265, no. 66), expresses his sense of the importance and of the weakness of Pendennis. He writes as follows :—There are two places in these western parts where, if not fortified, the enemy may easily prevail ; the harbours of Falmouth and Scilly, the one commanded by Pendennis, and the other by Hue Hill. If these can be kept, other places will be more difficult to attempt. If forced to front the enemy in these parts, there will be great want of powder and shot.

It appears probable that the third John Killigrew of Pendennis castle, continued captain of it until his death, and that he died about the year 1597.

He was succeeded by Sir Nicholas Parker, whose accession to the captain-ship may be taken to have been in about that year. Tonkin (in Carew, p. 359), makes him succeed immediately after Sir John Killigrew, who died in 1584. But, as we have seen, Sir John was succeeded in that year by his eldest son, who continued captain till about 1597.

The Queen, in a letter to Sir Nicholas Parker, dated Westminster, 4th Feb. 1598 (St. Pa. Dom. Ser. vol. 266, no 45), empowers him to exercise the charge of captain by deputy in case of necessity. She speaks also in this letter of the intended new fortifications at Pendennis, which, it is evident, had by this time been determined to be made upon an important scale. She writes to him as follows :—" By our patent we committed to you the charge of our fortifications intended to be built upon the haven of Falmouth, and made you colonel of certain foot companies appointed for its guard ; and, although in the said patent there is no warrant given you to exercise the charge of captain of the said fort by deputy, yet, if you find it necessary, for the safety of the country from spoils, upon the landing of any enemy there, to leave the fort and hold the field, with part of those companies under your charge, and such·other of our subjects as upon such occasion will be gathered together, you may commit the guard of the fort to two of the most ancient captains of companies there for the time, and employ yourself for our service elsewhere, as occasion shall require."

Sir Nicholas Parker subsequently appointed Nicholas Burton his deputy (See Carew, p. 359)

At the date of the Queen's letter, the works for the new fortifications at Pendennis were in progress. Sir Nicholas Parker, in a letter to Lord Burgley, dated Pendennis castle, the 27th Feb., 1598, writes :—"Since the beginning of our works here, I have followed Paul Ivey's directions to compass the ground to see how it will prove, and we find it somewhat rocky, which is like to be chargeable. You will perceive by the engineer's draft enclosed, that he has clean altered his plot, as he was mistaken in the ground, and for easing of the charge has made it less than Sir Fras. Godolphin and myself thought necessary. There are 400 workmen employed here, and our weekly charge is 80*l.*, besides emptions, so that I have very little money left, having received but 200*l.* to employ these, or more which might be had if money were beforehand. My duty binds me to acquaint you of the weakness and insufficiency of all things necessary for the defence of the castle. Upon my coming hither, I had but one piece of serviceable ordnance ; this above all is to be supplied, and many other matters fit for present service strengthened and amended, for which I hope to have allowance made." (St. Pa., Dom. Ser., vol. 266, no. 74). Paul Ivey, to whom the execution of the works appears to have been entrusted, writes to Lord Burgley, from Pendennis castle, on the 28th Feb., 1598 :—"At the works at Pendennis Hill, as much is weekly performed as is possible with 400 men. The circuit of the fort will be 200 perches, which may cost 6*l.* per perch, besides the emptions of wood to be employed in raising the work, and the repairing of tools." (St. Pa., Dom. Ser., vol. 266, no. 75). Norden alludes to the fortifications, which were erected at this period, and which still exist, where he says, " a peninsula lying poyntinge into the sea at ye mouth of *Falmouth* hauen, wherin K. Henr. the 8 buylded a Castle of stone; and since, Quen *Elizabeth* fortefyed it very stronglie with a very artificiall forte," (p. 50) : though it sounds strange to our modern ears, that bastions and connecting curtains built round-about a castle, should be called a " forte."

On the 18th October, 1598, a warrant was issued, to pay to Sir Nicholas Parker £46 13s. 4d., the monthly wages of 50 men in the new fort at Falmouth, from 7 October, to continue during pleasure (St. Pa., Dom Ser., Docquet, vol. 268, no 81) : this is 18s. 8d. for each man for a month, or 8d. a day.

On the 11th June, 1599, a warrant was issued, to pay to the Lieutenant of Ordnance, £191 10s. 1d. for provision of ordnance for Pendennis fort, and for carriage thither of the same, together with another proportion which was to be sent from the Tower. (St. Pa., Dom. Ser., Docquet, vol. 271, no. 7). On the 15th August, 1599, Sir Nicholas Parker wrote, from Pendennis castle, to Sir Walter Raleigh, Lord Warden of the Stannaries, &c., at Court, as follows : —" The ordnance, which, by letters of the whole Council, I was to receive from Mr. Vyvyan [the captain of St. Mawes castle] was denied me, and is since countermanded by two of the Council ; were it but one, I should in all humility have obeyed, although he disobeyed so many. Of all the ordnance which came down, I have but four pieces for defence of the front of the fort, which requires twelve at least. The castle of St. Mawes is impossible to be defended, and leaving the ordnance there, strengthens the enemy against us." (Vol. 272, no. 48). The next day he writes to Secretary Cecil:— " Thanks for your remembrance of my small strength, in a place so forlorn, and only 45 men allowed me, and not one officer." (Vol. 272, no. 49).

The following account given by Hals, of the fortifying, munifying, and garrisoning of Pendennis castle, is, as may be seen from the State Papers which I have above referred to, not very accurate. Hals, writing in about the year 1750, relates (p. 129), that Queen Elizabeth, " in her *Spanish* Wars, raised the new Fort and better'd the old Fortifications, as they are now extant. So that it is look'd upon as one of the most invincible Castles in this Kingdom, having [had] in it above 100 Pieces of Cannon mounted, and some Thousands of Foot Arms. After Queen ELIZABETH had thus fortified and munified the castle of *Pendenis*, she placed therein a band of 100 Soldiers, and over them placed, as her Governour, Sir *Nicholas Parker*, Kt."

Sir Nicholas Parker was colonel-general of the forces in Cornwall. Carew, writing in 1602, informs us (p. 212) that Sir Nicholas Parker's garrison at Pendennis, at that time, consisted of two companies of one hundred men each, of whom eighty were armed with muskets, sixty with calivers, and sixty were pikemen. He gives his estimate of other forces, and adds (p. 213):—" This may serve for a general estimate of the Cornish forces, which I have gathered, partly out of our certificate made to the Lords 1599, partly by information from the Serjeant Major, and partly through mine own knowledge."

In another passage (p. 362) he estimates the character of the governor in a very friendly spirit. He says:—" Howbeit (the) greatest strength [of Pendennis] consisteth in Sir Nicholas Parker, the governor, who demeaning himself no less kindly and frankly towards his neighbours, for the present, than he did resolutely and valiantly against the enemy when he followed the wars; therethrough commandeth, not only their bodies by his authority, but also their hearts by his love, to live and die in his assistance, for their common preservation, and her Highness' service."

It must have been this Sir Nicholas Parker, who appears to have made himself notorious by his fatal intimacy with that infamous syren, Lady Jane Killigrew, the wife of the last Sir John Killigrew, of Arwenack, grandson of the Sir John Killigrew, governor of Pendennis, mentioned above.

In Martin Killigrew's MS. history of the Killigrew's, as cited in the Journal of the Royal Institution of Cornwall, No. XII, April, 1871, p. 272, we find " The said last Sir John Killigrew, a sober good man, to his utter undoing, married ye daughter of an ancient and honourable family, now in ye peerage, in respect to whom I forbear the name; making herself infamous, and first debauched by ye Governor of Pendennis Castle."

This gay lady, who was a daughter of Sir George Fermor (p. 272, note), afterwards fell into trouble, which is thus related by Hals (p. 127):—" The Country People hereabout will tell you, that in the *Spanish* Wars, in the latter End of the Reign of Queen ELIZABETH, (Lady Jane) went aboard two *Dutch* Ships of the Hanse Towns, always free Traders in Times of War, driven into

Falmouth Harbour by cross Winds, laden with Merchandizes on Account (as was said) of *Spaniards*, and with a numerous Party of Ruffians slew the two *Spanish* Merchants, or Factors, on board the same, and from them took two Barrels, or Hogsheads, of *Spanish* Pieces of Eight, and converted them to her own Use. Now,......these Offenders were try'd and found Guilty, at *Lanceston*, of *Wilful Murder*, and had Sentence of Death passed accordingly upon them, and were all executed except the said Lady *Killigrew*, the principal Agent and Contriver of this barbarous Fact; who, by the Interest and Favour of Sir *John Arundell*, of *Tolverne*, Kt., and his Son-in-law Sir *Nicholas Hals*, of *Pengersick*, Kt. obtained of Queen ELIZABETH a Pardon, or Reprieve, for the said Lady, which was seasonably put into the Sheriff of *Cornwal*'s Hands." This was in Queen Elizabeth's reign, and therefore before 1603. Many years afterwards this Cornish Messalina was hospitably received by the corporation of Penryn, to whom, according to Hitchins and Drew (vol. 2, p. 291), she presented a silver cup bearing the following inscription :—" From maior to maior to the towne of Permarin (or Penryn), when they received me that was in great misery. J.K., 1633." But Hals says (p. 127), " This Lady *Jane Killigrew* afterwards gave a Silver Cup to the Mayors of *Penryn* for ever, in Memory of some Kindness in her Trouble received in that Corporation, 1612." And (p. 147) he gives the inscription thus " *From Mayor to Mayor, to the Town of* Penryn, *when they received me in great Misery*, Jane Killygrew, 1613." And these dates (1612 and 1613) agree. The cup was very massive, and was more than two feet high. The drawing of the cup is from a sketch by Miss Annie Shilson (Mrs. Quance, now unhappily deceased), in the 10th vol. of the Ham Anastatic Drawing Society.

The " great misery " referred to in Lady Jane's inscription, originated, according to Hitchins and Drew, in the scandalous outrage committed by her as above related; but I cannot agree with them in thinking so. The outrage was committed many years before the date of the gift. Davies Gilbert says (vol. 2, p. 21) this " horrible story cannot possibly be true, in the manner or to the extent in which it is related." And I do not believe it possible that the Mayor and Corporation received a gift occasioned and motived in the way suggested.

FROM MAIOR TO MAIOR
TO THE TOWNE OF PERMARIN
WHEN THEY RECEIVED MEE THAT
WAS IN GREAT MISERY.

Annie Quance.

Sir Nicholas Parker died in the year 1603.

In Budock church is the following inscription :—

D. O. M. Nicholas Parker, naturae munere generosae e stirpe eretus virtutis merito auratus eques creatuc ortu Sussexsiensis occasu Cornubiensis post plurimos pro Patria Principe pietate exantlatos labores his tandem quiescit.

$$\text{Anno} \quad \left\{ \begin{array}{c} \text{1537} \\ \text{1603} \end{array} \right\} \quad \text{vivere} \quad \left\{ \begin{array}{c} \text{cepit.} \\ \text{desit.} \end{array} \right.$$

Nicholaus Burton ejus in Praesidii Pendenisiani praefectura, vicarius obiens vices cique Propinquitatis amicitiae testamenti vere conjunctissimus perpetuae memoriae ergo moriens posuit.

Sir Nicholas Parker was succeeded in the government of Pendennis castle by John Parker, probably a son of Sir Nicholas. He is not named in the list of captains of the castle by any Cornish historian. Amongst the State Papers, however, is preserved irrefragable evidence of his captainship. The 20th May, 1603, is the date of the grant to John Parker of "the office of Keeper of Falmouth Castle" for life (St. Pa., Dom. Ser., vol. 1, no. 92, Ind. Wt. Bk., p. 2). John Parker may be supposed to have died in the year 1607.

In that year Sir John Parker, was appointed captain or keeper of Pendennis, or as it was then occasionally called, Falmouth castle. March, 1607, is the date of the grant to Sir John Parker of "the office of keeper of Falmouth Castle" for life. (St. Pa., Dom. Ser., vol. 26, no. 100, Ind. Wt. Bk., p. 56). He is not named in the list of captains by any of the Cornish historians. His captainship may be supposed to have continued to 1614. But there is room for some question, whether it did not determine somewhat earlier. In 1613, Sir Nicholas Hals (or Halse) appears to have been either governor or lieutenant-governor of the castle. Hals, the historian, and Gilbert and Tonkin speak of him as governor. But it appears certain, that he was not governor in the latter part of the year 1614, as Sir Robert Killigrew appears to have been appointed in July of that year. And a gazette sent by George Lord Carew to Sir Thomas Roe, speaks of Sir Robert Killigrew as succeeding Sir John Parker in the "Captainship of Falmouth." (St. Pa., Dom. Ser., vol. 95, no. 22). And if Sir John Parker, while governor, resided at a distance from the castle, and took little active part in its government, as, it is possible, may have been the case, his lieutenant may have been commonly regarded as for all practical purposes the governor, and even sometimes may have been addressed as governor in letters and other documents. And we may, perhaps, consider Sir Nicholas Hals to have been his lieutenant in 1613.

Sir Nicholas Hals, as lieutenant-governor or governor of Pendennis castle, was prominently connected with the rise into being, at about that date, of the town afterwards called Falmouth, and now grown into so great importance. There appear to have been then only a few dwellings at Smithicke and Penny-come-quicke, besides the manor house of the Killigrew family at Arwenack; and Mr. Killigrew proposed to build there a new town. (Hals, p. 128; Gilbert. vol. 2, p. 8; Carew, p. 358). He was met by jealous opposition on the part of Truro, Penryn and Helston, but in spite of this, King James I, in 1613, directed his privy counsellors, Hals tells us (p. 128), "to write to Sir *Nicholas Hals*, of *Fentongollan*, Kt. then Governor of *Pendenis Castle*, to be better inform'd of the true merits of this Case; and to know his own particular Sentiments about it." Sir Nicholas, "as soon as he received this Letter, made Answer, That he well approved of Mr. *Killigrew's* Project for building a Town and Custom-house at *Smithicke*, as being near the Mouth of the FAL Harbour; and briefly, amongst many others, for these Reasons especially: 1. For the quick and necessary Supply of such Ships, whose Occasions, or contrary Winds, brought them in there, without being obliged (as they then were) to go up Two Miles the River to *Penryn*, or nine miles to *Trurow*,......2. For the speedy supplying or reinforcing the Castle of *Pendenis*, contiguous therewith, with Men, Ammunition, and Provisions, in case of any Enemy's sudden Invasion, or endeavouring to take the same by Storm or Surprize, before the Country Militia could be raised, or Recruits brought in for that Purpose." (Hals, p. 128). The King thereupon decided in favour of Mr. Killigrew's project, and a town of comparative importance soon started into being.

Sir Robert Killigrew succeeded to the governorship of Pendennis castle in 1614. The 7th July in that year, is the date of the grant to him of "the office of Captain or Keeper of Pendennis Castle, for life." (St. Pa., Dom. Ser., vol. 77, no. 57; *Grant bk.*, p. 135). Not one of the historians of Cornwall names him in the list of governors.

Amongst the State Papers may be found (Dom. Ser., vol. 6, no. 137) a petition dated in the year 1625 (Sept. ?) from "the distressed soldiers of Pendennis Castle," to the King, which sets forth as follows :—A month ago they petitioned for their pay for 20 months, and order was given to the Lord

Treasurer to pay the same ; but their daily solicitations have been fruitless, and they have been forced to pawn their bedding and other necessaries to buy bread ; and they pray for an order for present payment for 21 months.

About two months later "the distressed soldiers of Pendennis Castle" petitioned the Council of War, and set forth as follows :—The petitioners, to the number of 50 men, should receive 8d. a day per man, but have not had any pay these two years, and are ready to perish for want of ordinary sustenance. They must of force forsake the garrison unless relieved. (Vol. 10, no. 69).

Capt. John Bonython wrote from Pendennis to Secretary Conway, on the 14th March, 1626, as follows :—The castle is entirely unprovided ; not one piece of ordnance mounted, nor have they a pound of shot. If lost, it would trouble the Kingdom to recover it, and what shame they should suffer if 5 or 6 ships were to come in, and send 200 or 300 men to burn and spoil the adjacent towns. (Vol. 22, no. 97). And again, on the 31st, as follows :— Various ships from Portugal, France and Spain have brought tidings that great preparations are making in the last mentioned country for an invasion of England.........Pendennis, instead of 40 pieces of ordnance, has not one mounted, and yet platforms ready for all. (Vol. 23, no. 106).

Captain John Bonython at this time was lieutenant-governor of Pendennis castle. It is certain, that he was not governor. Sir Robert Killigrew was governor. But captain John Bonython had command there, as we shall see presently. Sir Nicholas Hals, in 1626, was neither governor nor lieutenant-governor of the castle. The accounts given by Hals and Tonkin of the government of the castle at this period, are therefore widely inaccurate. Hals, after speaking of Sir Nicholas Parker as governor (p. 129), says (p. 130) ; "His Successor in the Government of this Castle was Sir *Nicholas Hals*, of *Fenton-gollan*, Knt., who died Governour thereof in 1637." The account of Tonkin (in Carew p. 359), is similar. In point of fact, Sir Nicholas Parker was succeeded in the governorship by John Parker, and he by Sir John Parker, and he by Sir Robert Killigrew, who remained governor for many years, and the probability appears to be, that Nicholas Burton, Sir Nicholas Parker's deputy, was succeeded in the lieutenant-governorship by Sir Nicholas Hals, and he, years before 1637, by Capt. John Bonython. Nicholas Burton, in a petition dated 1624, described himself as "late Lieutenant-Governor of Pendennis Fort." (St. Pa. Dom. Ser. vol. 168, No. 77). He probably had resigned the lieutenant-governorship, and been succeeded by Sir NicholasHals, in 1613.

In 1626 (April?), Sir John Killigrew wrote to Secretary Conway, and appealed to him to remove Captain John Bonython from the command of Pendennis castle, on account of his misconduct, principally of a private and personal nature against Sir John. (St. Pa. Dom. Ser., vol. 25, No. 102).

A petition of Sir Robert Killigrew, captain of Pendennis castle, to the Council of War, in 1626, (April?), sets forth as follows :—Petitioner has been a suitor for ten years for a supply for the castle and alterations in the fortifica-tions. For 9 years there has not been a piece of ordnance mounted, and at this time there are not above 4 barrels of powder. He prays for repairs, and also that the garrison of 50 men may have their pay, which they have been 2 years without. " Had they not lived on limpets (a poor kind of shell-fish), without bread or any other sustenance," save some small relief from the petitioner, they had all been starved. (Vol. 25, No. 105).

Capt. John Bonython in a letter from Pendennis, dated the 26th May, 1626, to Secretary Conway, mentions, that on his return to the fort, he finds the south bulwark fallen down. He speaks also of the continued malice of Sir John Killigrew, who desires to remove Bonython, and to get himself appointed. (Vol. 27, No. 73). In another letter from Pendennis to Secretary Conway, dated the 22nd Oct., 1626, he speaks of the distressed condition of himself and his soldiers for want of pay. (Vol. 38, No. 39). And in another, dated the 26th Nov., 1626, he calls attention to the defenceless condition of Pendennis : not a gun mounted, nor scarcely any ammunition ; and the soldiers in great misery, having had no money for three years. (Vol. 40, No. 29).

A petition of Sir Robert Killigrew, captain of Pendennis castle, to the Council, dated the 12th Jan., 1627, sets forth as follows :—The petitioner has wearied the Board with 69 several petitions during 11 years, importuning a supply for the fort, and an order for the soldiers' pay, which is now 2¾ years in arrear. He prays an order for the latter object, some of the soldiers having already perished for want. All other forts have received some help. (Vol. 49, no. 6). It would be as surprising as it is painful, to find that these poor soldiers were so long and shamefully neglected as they were, if it were not known, that the Exchequer was at the time impoverished by the foolish and fruitless war with Spain. It is both painful and surprising, to find a warrant dormant, dated the 3rd April, 1627, to give order to the receiver general of the revenues of Devon and Cornwall, to pay to Sir Robert Killigrew, captain of Pendennis castle, 638*l.* 15*s.* per ann., for 50 men more to be added for defence thereof (Docquet, vol. 59, no. 17); and a warrant of the same date to pay to Sir Robt. Killigrew and Sir Francis Godolphin, 1,117*l.*, and 800*l.* imprest, for repairing Pendennis castle, for new fortifications to be made there, and for repairing the fort of St. Mary's, Island of Scilly. (Docquet, vol. 59, no. 17). On the 6th Aug., 1627, Sir Robert wrote from Pendennis to Secretary Conway, and informed him, that they had wrought three weeks on the repairs of the fortifications at Pendennis; reported the results, and suggested alterations at an additional expense of 300*l.* (Vol. 73, no. 49). It may be charitably, and perhaps probably conjectured, that the distressed soldiers received their pay at about this time.

Sir Robert Killigrew remained the sole governor of Pendennis castle until the 21st March, 1628.

His son, Sir William Killigrew, whose name, as well as his father's, is omitted by all the historians of Cornwall in their lists of governors, was from that date for several years, associated with Sir Robert Killigrew in the governorship. The 21st March, 1628, is the date of the grant made to Sir Robert Killigrew and Sir William Killigrew, his son, of the offices of captain of the fort at Pendennis, and colonel of 100 men there, for their lives, with survivorship, with a fee of 10s. per diem for the captain, 46*l.* 13*s.* 4*d.* for 50 of the soldiers, [*i.e.*, for a month's wages, at 8d. a day each man], and 638*l.* 15*s.* for the other 50 lately appointed, [*i.e.*, for a year's wages, at 9d. a day each man], and 40*l.* per annum for reparation of the fort. ([Coll. Sign Man., Car. I, Vol. 6, no. 62]. Vol. 96, no. 65).

John Tresahar, who was probably lieutenant-governor of Pendennis castle in 1628, (he certainly was in 1636—see St. Pa. Dom. Ser. vol. 321, no. 16), wrote, from Pendennis, to Sir Robert Killigrew, on the 10th April in that year, and informed him, that Hannibal Bonython, Sir Francis Vivian's lieutenant at St. Mawes, troubled the harbour, by forcing the captains of ships to present themselves at that castle. (Vol. 104, no. 38). On this subject there arose a memorable dispute between the castles, as will be seen presently.

A certificate by William, Earl of Pembroke, dated the 22nd Aug., 1628, shows the strength of the garrison of the fort at Pendennis, as found at a general muster, to have been :—armed men, 394 ; pioneers, 99. (Vol. 113, no. 55).

The "difference" between the castles had become more serious about the end of the year 1630. In a petition of "Sir William Killigrew, captain of Pendennis castle, to the Lords of the Admiralty," the date of which was probably in that year, Sir William complains, that Hannibal Bonithon, lieutenant to Sir Francis Vivian, in the castle of St. Mawes, has for the last two years compelled all ships to stay at the castle of St. Mawes, and to make certain declarations as to their passengers and commissions, which have been accustomed to be made at Pendennis castle only. This practice, says Sir William, was condemned by their Lordships two years ago, but is still continued in contempt. He prays that Sir Francis Vivian, or Hannibal Bonithon may be sent for. (Vol. 181, no. 5). Hannibal Bonithon was sent for accordingly. And after both sides had been heard, the Lords of the Admiralty, on the 6th May, 1631, made their order, "in the difference between the castles of Pendennis and St. Mawes." This was their order. Pendennis is to call to account ships which anchor on the west side, and St. Mawes, those which anchor on the east side of the Black Rock. (Vol. 190, no. 33).

Against this order, however, Sir William Killigrew, on the 2nd July, 1631, presented a petition to the King. The Lords of the Admiralty, says Sir William, having taken away the ancient privileges of the fort of Pendennis in the harbour of Falmouth, and given equal command to St. Mawes, a block house, to which there are but 16 men allowed ; he prays that His Majesty would stay that order, and hear what the petitioner can say thereon.

The petition is underwritten as follows :—The King, having declared his purpose to hear these differences himself, directs the execution of the order above mentioned to be stayed in the meantime. Greenwich, 1631, July 2, (vol. 196, nos. 7, and 7. I).   But I do not find that the King did hear the differences, or that any order, after this interim order, was ever made.

In 1632, the garrison of Pendennis, which had been increased from 50 to 100 men in the year 1628, was reduced again to 50.   This reduction was not approved of by Sir Robert Killigrew, and he on the 11th June, 1632, wrote a letter on this subject to the Council of War.   In this letter, he expressed his opinion of the ill policy of the reduction, and he observed upon the importance of the fort, the inadequacy of the garrison, and the small amount of saving to be effected by the reduction ; and if they determined to make it, he desired that his protestation might be kept.   (Vol. 218, no. 34).

A letter, the date of which was probably in 1634, from Thomas Lord Arundel, of Wardour, to the Council, contains an account of "the ruins of Pendennis Castle," with a request to the Council to take the same into consideration ; Pendennis, continues the writer, being the only defence of one of the most considerable harbours in England.   (Vol. 281, no. 56).

Sir Robert Killigrew died on the 26th Nov., 1633.   (Bibl. Corn.)

Sir William Killigrew was sole captain of the castle from that date till April, 1635.

Sir William Killigrew, on or shortly before the 17th April, 1635, surrendered the captainship of Pendennis castle.   (See St. Pa. Dom. Ser., vol. 288, no. 94). He died in Oct., 1695.   (Bibl. Corn.)

CHAPTER III.

SIR William Killigrew's successor in the government of Pendennis castle, was Sir Nicholas Slanning. He was appointed by letters patent of the king, dated the 17th April, 1635. (St. Pa., Dom. Ser., vol. 288, no. 94). John Tresahar was his lieut.-governor. (Vol. 321, no. 16).

On the 25th February, 1639, Sir Nicholas Slanning received instructions from the king, to take ordnance, ammunition and men from " Falmouth port," on a secret expedition for the king to Cumberland. (St. Pa., Dom. Ser., vol. 413, no. 88.) What may have been the object of this secret expedition, does not appear. It was the time of the Scots' troubles, and possibly Sir Nicholas Slanning was to have taken part in subduing the Scots.

We come now to the unhappy period of the civil war in England. Hallam says, (vol. 2, p. 150, 10th edit.) "with evil auspices, with much peril of despotism on the one hand, with more of anarchy on the other, amidst the apprehensions and sorrows of good men, the civil war commenced in the summer of 1642."

Unquestionably when the chivalry of England, with heavy hearts and much uncertainty, chose sides, there were many high-minded and earnest men of both parties, with whose conflicting feelings we cannot but all sympathize. Some held, that the king's triumph would be the death of national freedom, and maintained the legal right on the part of subjects illegally treated, to resist such treatment ; whilst many feared lest monarchy should be entirely destroyed by parliamentary power. Nearly all wished for the preservation of the monarchy in some shape or other ; at the beginning, only a very few advanced thinkers dreamed of a republic. The feelings possessing the minds of many earnest and honourable men at that time, may be illustrated in the persons of the gallant Sir William Waller on the one side, and Sir Henry Slingsby on the other. Neither of these brave Englishmen thought the worse of friends who took the side hostile to his own. Waller wrote to Sir Ralph Hopton, " Hostility itself cannot violate my friendship to your person, but I must be true to the cause wherein I serve." Waller called God to witness the hatred he had of entering upon what he touchingly designated as " a war without an enemy," and he adds in reference to the parts which he and Sir Ralph had to act " *in this tragedy*," " Let us do it in a way of honour, and without personal animosities." (Pol., vol. iv., p. 98, note). Sir Henry Slingsby expressed similar sentiments, when he, among others, was first called on by the king, (whom he served loyally, and for whom he suffered death upon the scaffold), to raise forces against the Scots. Slingsby went on to Braham moor to see some light horse, there levied and exercised, and he mournfully calls it the " spectacle of our public death." He writes, " It is, I say, a thing horrible that we should engage ourselves in war one with another, and with our venom gnaw and consume ourselves."

In the midst of the general ferment which prevailed throughout the nation, Cornwall presented a petition to the house of commons, soliciting a redress of grievances. Among these grievances the petition set forth that the castles of St. Mawes and Pendennis were much decayed in their fortifications ; and that the harbours of Fowey and Helford had been left without means of defence. The petitioners therefore prayed, that the former might be speedily repaired, and that the value of the latter might be taken into consideration ; that such measures might be adopted as would put the county into a respectable state of defence. The parliament calculated upon meeting with little opposition to their measures from any Cornish fortress except Pendennis castle, the captain of which, Sir Nicholas Slanning, was well known to be in the interest of the king. (Pol., vol. iv, p. 97).

In 1643, the defeat of the parliamentary forces was so decisive in the memorable battle of Stratton, that the war was driven for several months away from Cornwall. In Somersetshire the Cornish reaped fresh laurels, at Lansdown and at the siege of Bristol, where St. Nicholas Slanning and Col. John Trevanion were slain. Of these brave young officers Lord Clarendon observes, that "they were the life and soul of the Cornish regiment, neither of them exceeded twenty-eight, their friendship for each other was unbounded and entire." These heroes, with Sir Beville Grenville, had raised companies of volunteers among the Cornish, and led them to victory in the royal cause. (Pol., vol. iv, p. 98). Sir Nicholas Slanning's death was on the 6th July, 1643. He is referred to in the following distich, cited on p. xvii of Murray's Handbook for Devon and Cornwall.

> The four wheels of Charles's wain,
> Grenville, Godolphin, Trevanion, Slanning, slain.

On the death of Sir Nicholas Slanning, the king appointed to the governorship of Pendennis castle, Col. John Arundel, of Trerise in Newlyn. His unalterable attachment to the royal cause, procured for him the name of "*John for the King.*" He was M.P. for Cornwall in Queen Elizabeth's reign, and "when she was encamped there with her Army, in expectation of the *Spaniards* Landing, 1588" (Hals, p. 130), and was called "*Old Tilbury,*" in consequence; or as Polwhele says, "was at the battle (?) of Tilbury, whence his nickname." In 1643, when he was appointed governor of Pendennis castle, John Arundel was sixty-seven, some accounts say, eighty-seven years of age. Tonkin says, that this "John Arundel and his mother-in-law lived to a very great age." (Pryce's MS).

Who was lieutenant-governor of Pendennis castle under Arundel, admits of some doubt. Col. Lewis Tremayne, of Heligan, certainly held some position of importance at the castle during John Arundel's governorship; and some of his descendants now living at Heligan, believe him to have been lieutenant-governor. But there are also grounds for supposing that Richard Arundel, the eldest son of the governor, may have been his lieutenant. Certainly he was with him in the castle; and Sir William Killigrew, the former governor, who, as we have seen, resigned the governorship in 1635, was, in January, 1643, desirous that the reversion of the government, after John Arundel, should be bestowed on his son Richard Arundel, and petitioned the king accordingly. The king wrote a letter in reply, which now is in the possession of J. Rashleigh, Esq., of Menabilly, and to his courtesy I am indebted for a copy of it. The letter is addressed, " To Sir William Killigrew," and is as follows :—

Will Killigrew.

Your suite unto me that I would conferre upon Mr. Arundell of Trerise Eldest sonne the reversion after his father of the government of Pendennis Castle which I had formerly bestowed upon you, is so great a testimonye of your affection to my service & of your preferring the good of that before any Interest of your owne that I have thought fitt to lett you knowe in this particulai way, how well I take it & that my conferring that place according to your desire shall bee an earnest unto you of my intentions to recompence & reward you in a better (kinde ?)

restinge   Your assured frend

Oxford the 12th   CHARLES R.
Jan : 1643.

So soon after the appointment of John Arundel to the governorship as July 1644, he testified to his unfaltering loyalty, by harbouring at Pendennis castle, his queen, Henrietta Maria. Polwhele says (vol. iv., p. 98, note AA.), " The 16th of June in Exon, she was delivered of the illustrious Princess Henrietta Maria. But the poor Queen was forced thence the next Sunday [the 23rd.] Frighted by Essex she went in her litter for Cornwall." The parliamentary army, under the earl of Essex, was pursuing her. She hastened to Pendennis, where some Dutch vessels, sent thither by the prince of Orange for her service, were ready to transport her swiftly into France. (Clar. Hist. Rebel., bk. viii, par. 84).

The following from the sheriff of Cornwall to Mrs. Basset, written presumably at the time of the queen's flight to Pendennis castle, suggests the 3rd or 4th of July as probably the day on which she was received there. (See Lake, vol. iv, Supp. p. 5 ; and see Lyson, vol. 3, p. 104.)

This thyrd of July 1644.

Deare Wiffe, ...Here is the woefullest spectacle my eyes yet ever look'd on ; the most worne and weak pitifull creature in ye world, the poore Queene shifting for one hour's liffe longer.

The queen, according to Agnes Strickland's account (vol. 5, p. 314, edition 1851), which probably in this particular is correct, remained only one night in Pendennis castle, and sailed early the following morning, in a Dutch vessel, for France. Agnes Strickland gives the 29th June as the date. The queen, according to Polwhele (iv, 98, note AA.), "arrived at Brest, the 5th of July, 1644." One of the "king's pamphlets," entitled "A true Relation of the Queen's Departure from Falmouth into the Brest in the West of France. Lond. July 22, 1644", relates, that "the designe of her expedition could not bee carried with so much secrecy, but it vvas discovered to the Lord Admirall, who on the first information of it, knovving of what consequence was her departure into France, did command all the ships then in the westerne parts to overtake her : they could not (at the first command) come so easily as vvas desired, but having knowledge of what importance was the businesse, vvith Wind and sayle they made haste to overtake her. And indeed had the Wind bin more propitious to them, they had gone neer to have possessed themselves of this mighty prize." There follows in the same pamphlet, a letter giving details of the pursuit, and of the firing at the queen's vessel. This pamphlet gives as the date of the queen's departure, the 14th July.

The diary of a royalist Essex gentleman, Mr. Richard Symons, who accompanied the king, as one of his lieutenants, through the campaign, informs us that previous to the battle of Broadoak, viz., on Monday, 26 August, 1644, "Also this day came to us 100 barrels of powder, &c., from Pendennis Castle." (Lake, vol. iv., Supp. p. 13).

It was in this year (1644), that the duke of Hamilton was sent to Pendennis castle, to be detained a prisoner there. He had by his unaccountable conduct given cause for his loyalty to be suspected, and the king, "to prevent his doing further mischief," had him sent "in custody to the castle of Bristol, and from thence to Exeter, and so to the castle at Pendennis in Cornwall." (Clar. Hist. Rebel. bk. vii, par. 408). According to Lyson (vol. 3, p. 104), the duke was imprisoned there during 1644 and the following year. And it appears from Clarendon's account, that the duke was not removed thence, until "about the month of November" in the year 1645. (Bk. ix, par. 158).

Afterwards he acted "a great part for the King," and was general in the head of a great army. (par. 154.)

Towards the end of August, 1645, the chancellor (Sir E. Hyde), was sent by the prince to Pendennis castle, "under pretence of giving some direction in the matter of the customs, but in truth to take care that the frigate provided for the prince's transportation might be in readiness, and victual to be privately made ready, to be presently put on board when the occasion should require." (Cl. Hist. Reb. bk. ix, par. 79).

On the 8th Oct., 1645, Lord Norwich wrote from Havre to Sir E. Hyde, who was then at Pendennis castle. He says :—He will be with him in a few days, if he can pass through the parliamentary forces. With great professions of affection, he renews his propositions, sent by his servant, for the government of Pendennis castle ; if they are not entertained, he has discharged his duty, and will write on the gate as he passes, that you can have no more of a cat than his skin. He urges most strongly, that the prince be not sent to France. He has read seven romances of ten volumes to make him valiant enough to relieve Exeter. If he can only get Orandates and Arsace over with him, he is made, and England saved. If he is not to have Pendennis, he will steer his course some other way, where he may hope to do the king service, and not follow after him with his thumbs in his girdle. (Clar. St. Pa. no. 1987). And on the 18th or 28th of the same month, he writes a further letter from Havre to Sir E. Hyde, pressing his propositions for the command of Pendennis, with extravagant professions of attachment to his sweet, dear, young master, with the king and queen, on whom his soul dotes, &c. (No. 2008). It does not appear, that the propositions of Lord Norwich for the government of Pendennis, were entertained. And as we have seen, the king had already bestowed the reversion of the government after John Arundel, upon his son Richard Arundel.

On the 29th Oct., 1645, the prince of Wales wrote to Lord Hopton and Sir E. Hyde, who were then at Pendennis, and directed them, to put the castle in order for his highness's reception and abode there the ensuing winter. (Clar. St. Pa. no. 2010).

On the 2nd Nov., 1645, the prince at Liskeard issued a warrant to the governor of Pendennis, ordering an addition to the garrison. (No. 2015).

The duke of Hamilton was removed from Pendennis for two reasons : one, that "it was enough foreseen that the prince himself might be put to a retreat to Pendennis-castle" (Cl. Hist. Reb. ix, par. 158), and it was not thought fit that he should reside there with him, who was so much in the king's displeasure : the other, that "many good men" were solicitous regarding the influence the duke had with the governor, "of which there was so universal a suspicion, that many letters were writ to the council, that if he were not speedily disposed to some other place, they feared the castle would be betrayed : and sir Richard Greenvil writ earnestly to the prince about it, and sir Harry Killigrew (a person of entire affection to the king, and a true friend of the governor) very importunately. So that about the month of November, the king's warrant for his removal was sent to sir Arthur Basset, governor of the Mount; who went to Pendennis in the morning, and took him with him to the Mount, in order to removing him to Scilly, when the time should require it; the duke expressing great trouble and discontent that he should be removed, and the governor, and all that family and garrison, made show of no less grief to part with him, he having begotten a great opinion in that people of his integrity and innocence" (par. 158).

The prince was very much troubled at a letter he received from Sir Richard Greenvil, near the end of November, 1645, "and the more" "because he [the prince] had discerned that [Sir Richard Greenvil] laboured very much to infuse a jealousy into the governor of Pendennis-castle, that the prince intended to remove him from that command, and to confer it upon the Lord Hopton; to which purpose [Sir Richard] had written to [the governor] from Okington, (when the Lord Hopton and the chancellor were sent down [to Pendennis castle] to assist him in the fortifying and supplying that castle ; which if they had not [done,] it could not have held out, as it did afterwards), that the lord Hopton had a commission to take that charge from him ; but that [the governor] should not suffer such an affront to be put upon him ; for [Sir Richard] and all [the governor's] friends would stick to him in it :

whereas there was never the least thought or intention to make any alteration in that government." (Clar. Hist. Rebel. vol. 4, par. 104).

The subjoined letter is said by Polwhele (vol. 4, p. 100), to have been written to Col. Ciely, "then at Pendennis Castle." Polwhele says : "The original is among the family papers of the Rev. George Moore, of Grampound, who very obligingly copied it, for my purpose." The Parochial History of Cornwall, published by Lake, (vol. iv, supp. p. 25), gives the letter with this heading, "Cromwell to Colonel Ciely at Pendennis Castle." But this heading does not appear in Polwhele, and so, no doubt, the letter itself was not so headed. This then is the letter.

December 10th, 1645, Teverton.

Sr,

Its the deseir of Sr. Gilbert Pickeringe that his deceased Brother Col. Pickering should bee enterred in your guarrison, And to the end his funeral may bee sollemnized with as much Honor as his memorie calls for, you are desired to give all possible assistance therein, the particulars will be offered to you by his Maior, Maior Gubbs, with whome I deseir you to concurr herein ; and believe itt sir you will not only lay a huge obligation upon myselfe and all the officers of this Armie, but I dare assure you the General himselfe will take, it for an especial favor and will not lett it goe without a full acknowledgment. But what neede I prompt him to soe honourable an action whose owne ingenuitye wil be argument sufficient heerin, whereof rests assured your humble servant

OLIVER CROMWELL.

Was Col. Ciely "then at Pendennis Castle," as Polwhele supposes ? There are letters preserved amongst the Clarendon State Papers, one from Col. Slingsby at Pendennis, dated the 23rd Dec., 1645 (No. 2055), and one from John Arundel at Pendennis castle, dated the 24th Dec., 1645 (No. 2058), both of them written to Lord Clarendon himself (then Sir E. Hyde), which distinctly negative any such supposition, as that the parliamentary troops, in December, 1645, had temporary occupation of Pendennis castle. Nor is it probable, that Col. Ciely was a royalist and under Arundel at Pendennis castle, and that Col. Pickeringe was a prisoner of war there. Col. Ciely is not named in the list presently referred to, of the garrison in 1646. We may suppose, therefore, that he was in command of some other castle (or "guarrison") than Pendennis castle, in December, 1645.

In January or February 1646, Sir E. Hyde wrote to Mr. Secretary Nicholas, that Pendennis castle was victualled for a year, and they would soon retreat there. (No. 2108.)

The prince, who "came to Truro on the 12th day of February" (1646), (Clar. Hist. Rebel. bk. ix. par. 145), "having stayed some days at Truro, went to Pendennis; intending only to recreate himself for two or three days, and to quicken the works, which were well advanced; his highness having issued all the money he could procure towards them, and colonel Slingsby intending them with great diligence and activity.   But in the very morning that he meant to return to Truro, [his] army being then retired, and Fairfax at the edge of Cornwall, the lord Hopton and the lord Capel sent advertisements, that they had severally received intelligence of a design to seize the person of the prince; and that many persons of quality of the country were privy to it.   Hereupon the prince thought it most convenient to stay where he was, and so returned no more to Truro.   The time of apparent danger was now in view, and if there were in truth any design of seizing the prince's person, they had reason to believe that some of his own servants were not strangers to it."   (Bk. ix., par. 147.)

It was probably at about this date, if ever, that the prince, suspecting, as has been seen, his own servants, who were in the castle, retired into the room there, which still retains the name of the king's room.   We read, (Hitch. and Drew, vol. 2., p. 256.): "There is still a room in this castle, which retains the name of the king's room; and in a closet over, there was formerly a small fire-place, about twelve inches square.   In this closet, according to tradition, Charles was concealed.   This, and a vacancy for a seat opposite the fire-place, were demolished [about 1808,] when this part of the Castle underwent some repairs."

Amongst the Clarendon State Papers, there is a draught proposal by the prince, dated Feb. 1646, Pendennis, to erect a chapel in the castle.   In this paper (no. 2133), the prince rehearses his motives for dedicating a place of worship within the garrison, invites contributions, and directs that this resolution and request should be published in all churches and chapels in the Duchy, and that contributors' coats of arms should be fixed up in the chapel, and that Lionel Gatford, chaplain to the garrison, should receive and pay monies.

After the battle of Torrington, (16th Feb., 1646,) "Sir Ralph Hopton fled into Cornwall with the remnant of his force, sending the news to the Prince of Wales and his Council at Pendennis Castle, where the greatest consternation prevailed." (Life of the great Lord Fairfax, p. 265.)   Lord Clarendon's account is, that "the lords Hopton and Capel" sent advices to Pendennis, to the effect, that it was not fit to venture his highness any longer "in that castle, (which would not only not preserve his person, but probably, by his stay there, might be lost; which by his absence might defend itself,) and that he should remove to Jersey or Scilly." (Clar. Hist. Rebel. bk. ix. par. 148.) "The next morning, being Monday the second of March," "the governor and his son were called into the Council [at Pendennis castle], and made acquainted with the prince's resolution that night to embark himself for Scilly, being a part of Cornwall; from whence, by such aids and relief as he hoped he should procure from France and foreign parts, he should be best able to relieve them. And accordingly that night, about ten of the clock, he put himself aboard, and on Wednesday in the afternoon by God's blessing arrived safe in Scilly." (Bk. ix. par 149.)

It is interesting to see the accounts given of the prince's embarkation in different news-letters printed in a newspaper of the period.   The "Perfect Diurnal" (no. 136,) has news "out of the VVest," by a letter of the 3rd of March, that "the Prince is in *Pendennis* Castle, expecting a wind for *France*, the Country generally hate them, and rise for us;" but adds, "Besides this former, there be other letters come to the Speaker and other Members of Parliament, certainly affirming that the Prince is gone to Sea, with the Lord *Capel*, L. *Culpepper*, *Ned Hide*, and many others of quality in company, there being three ships of them in all, whereof one of them upon the first setting out, viz., Sunday night last *March* 1, it being a tempestuous night, was cast away in sight of Land; . . . . the Prince and Company with the other two ships are gone for Silly *Island* (as tis said)."

On the 9th March, 1646, Sir Ralph Hopton, having previously sent his infantry and a considerable part of his ammunition to Pendennis castle and St. Michaels mount, capitulated his cavalry to Sir Thomas Fairfax, who at this time had the command of the parliamentary forces in the west.

Thereupon some of the parliamentary party imagined that Pendennis castle would forthwith surrender on moderate conditions. In a newspaper, ("A Perfect Diurnall,") for the 16th to the 23rd of March, is printed a letter dated "Truro, March 11," in which the writer, after speaking of the treaty which is in progress with the Lord Hopton for the disbanding of his forces, says, "We doubt not, but Pendennis will upon the disbanding of these Forces, incline to moderate terms, the Governour thereof is a Gentleman of good Fortune and Estate in the Country, and in all likelyhood will not be so mad to see all the whole Gentry at liberty, injoying their owne, and himself as it were in prison, injoying nothing that is his own. I cannot express with what joy most of the Officers receive those conditions, and wish they had sooner known our intentions towards them."

On the 14th of March, according to Whitelock, (p. 197,) "a hundred and twenty Musqueteers armed, came out of *Pendennis* Castle, and yielded themselves to Sir *Thomas Fairfax.*"

Col. Arundel, in anticipation of the coming of the parliament forces to establish themselves before Pendennis at Pennycomequicke, and at Arwenack house as head quarters, sallied forth from the castle on the 16th of March, and would have burned both the house and the town ; but the enemy coming somewhat earlier than was expected, the soldiers of the castle succeeded only in burning a great part of the manor house. This is that ancient mansion of the Killigrews, which we are told, (Hitch. and Dr., vol. 2, p. 258), was, in 1567, esteemed the finest and most costly in the county. Tonkin, (in Gilb. vol. 2, p. 18, and in Carew, p. 359), and Polwhele (vol. 4, p. 101, note x), credit Sir John Killigrew with having, with his own hands, set fire to it, in order that the enemy "might not find shelter in it." And Hitchins and Drew say, (vol. 2, p. 258), "this house was set on fire ; but whether by Sir John Killegrew, its owner, who was a zealous royalist, to prevent it from falling into the hands of the adverse party, or by the malice of the governor of Pendennis Castle, under that pretext, is rather uncertain. A manuscript history of the Killigrew family asserts the former." It is the latter which is asserted in the extract from a copy of the manuscript history given below; and it appears that Sir John Killigrew died in 1636, (see Bibl. Corn.), and that, in 1646, his widow, although she had been divorced, held the property.   The account given by the Killigrew MS., as cited in the Journal of the Royal Institution of Cornwall for April, 1871, No. XII, p. 275, is as follows:—"In the year 1648, ye said infamous Lady Jane died.   (Sir Peter came into his estate,) but came not time enough to prevent ye malicious and envious Governor of Pendennis from burning his fine house of Arwenack, upon Sir William Waller's (Oliver's general) coming to besiege ye Castle."   The Killigrew MS. was written many years after the burning.   The governor of Pendennis intended to burn not the house only, but the town also, as appears in a cotemporaneous account, in a letter signed "T.M.," which will be cited presently.   The imputation of envious and malicious motives to the governor, in reference to an act which appears to have been simply strategical and defensive, appears to have been made under a misapprehension of the facts.

On the 17th of March, Sir Thos. Fairfax had quartered two regiments in Pennycomequicke : and he himself, with the best of his party, was established in the part of Arwenack house, which they had saved from the burning, the day previous.   With these two regiments, they intended to block up the castle on the land side.

The "Perfect Diurnal" for the 16th to the 23rd March, prints a letter which had been read in the house of Commons on the 19th March.   The letter contains the following :—"For the Castle of *Pendennis*, I make no doubt as soon as this Army is totally disbanded (which though it begin to morrow, will take two or three days before it be ended, make what speed we can) we shall find them tractible ; if not, we shall settle this Country in such a posture of Security against that place, as will compell them in a short time to hearken to worse Propositions then they now might have had, if they persist in a refusall of the Summons intended to be sent them."   This letter was written probably on or about the 17th March.

A very interesting letter "From Truro the 19th of March, 1645," (i.e., 1646), and signed "T.M.," is printed in a pamphlet printed "March 26, 1646," and entitled "Sir Thomas Fairfaxes taking of Dennis Castle, &c., with the Generalls summons sent in to Pendennis Castle, &c."   From this letter I extract the following :—"The Fort on the East side of the harbour of

Faymouth, and right over against *Pendennis* Castle [i.e. St. Mawes Fort] is yeelded up by *Bowthan* (that was the Lieutenant thereof) unto the General five dayes since, who hath placed a very strong Garrison in it . . . . Yesterday . . . . *Dennis* Castle . . . . was yeelded up . . . . it will prove to be of very great use to us, for the taking in of *Pendennis*, by meanes that our ships lying there, may prevent (by the helpe of St. *Mawes*) the conjunction of any ships for the reliefe thereof : I went with the Generall and the Committee to receive the possession of this Fort, and in the way the Generall went unto *Arwinkle*, Sir *Peter Killegrew's* house, where and in the Village of *Pennicomquicke* we had quartered two Regiments for the blocking up of *Pendennis* Castle on the land side. The day before the Generall sent thither those two Regiments, the enemie in the Castle set on fire Sir *Peters* house, and burned a great part therof downe to the ground, and would have done the like with *Pennicomequicke*, had not our mens unexpected comming prevented them in the Castle . . . . the man of War that hath 40 pieces of Ordnance in him which lyeth a ground on the North side of the Fort let us passe very quietly through *Pennicomquicke*, and to *Arwinkle*, which lyes within half musket shot of the enemies Out-workes but is blinded by the houses and trees, so that they cannot see those that are on the other side of the house; but when we came off and were past *Pennicomequicke*, and advanced into an open field in our way backe to *Perin*, the ship that lay on the North side of the Castle let flye at us, but their shot (by God's mercy) did us no harme, though the bullets flew very neer us, and one grazed not far from mee, which wee found, and was a bullet of some 12 l. weight. As soon as the Generall came to *Perin* he caused a summons to be drawne up, and sent it by his Drum-Major unto the Governour of the Castle, requiring him to yeeld it unto him for the use of the Parliament, using divers reasons to perswade him thereunto; But *Arundell* of *Treverse* who is the Governour thereof, gave him a peremptory denyall, saying, that hee was 70 years old, and could not have many dayes to live, and therefore would not in his old years blemish his honour in surrendering thereof, and would be rather found buried in the ruines thereof, than commit so vilde a Treason, (or words to that effect). Questionlesse the place is very strong, as well by its naturall scituation, (it being almost an Island, and seated on a rising hill) as by Art and great industry ; and it is victualled (as they say) for nine or ten moneths, and they have in it about one thousand or twelve hundred men, all desperate persons, and good souldiers ; and they have powder and shot great store, and at least eighty great Guns mounted, besides forty in the ship which lies on the North side of the Castle. Therefore the Generall resolves to block it up very close both by Land and Sea : which hee may the better doe, in regard that we have *Denis* Castle, and the Haven of *Helford* on the west, and St. *Maws* on the east; and for that, if we draw a line thwart the narrow necke of Land, a little on this side *Arwinkle* house, which is not above Musquet shot over : *Pendenis* Castle will remaine unto them but as a close and sure prison, and so in the end the belly will conquer them, without striking of a stroake. Here are in this Fort many very considerable men, and the most desperate Persons, and the violentest enemies that the Parliament hath in this kingdom : and the Country reports, they have a very great masse of wealth in this Castle, for this was ever a place the enemy did much confide in : I verily beleeve that if the Workes were once perfected for blocking of them up, two thousand good foote would keep them in, that they should not be able to break forth to annoy the Countrey. *Penicomquicke* and *Peryne* will be able to entertain that number very well. . . . . This last night one of the ships which came down with Sir *George Askew*, fell into the Harbour of *Falmouth*, on St. *Mawes* side, and notwithstanding both the Block-house, and the Bulwarke at the poynt of *Pendennis* shot very furiously at her, yet she came very safely into the Harbour, and so passed upon the Tide, to a place in the harbour called *Mawpasse* passage, where a Frigot of Dunkerks had run herselfe aground and [which] came in on purpose to assist *Pendennis* Castle, she had in her 26 pieces of Ordnance, and though our men entered her, yet she stood very stoutly to her defence, yet at last we masterd her, and took all the men out of her, and put in her about fifty men of our owne, and so intend to make her a Man of Warre to serve the State, and she may prove very usefull, for she is an exceeding good sailer, and will bee good against our enemies Navigable ships, that so we may take them. Sir, most of the great Malignants of the Countrey (unlesse those that are in *Pendennis* and the Mount) are come in ; If you alone do not take some speedy course to remove them out of the

County, untill the County bee fully setled, I feare it will not bee long before we shall have new troubles here. Thus with the tendernesse of my best love and service I rest,

Yours in what ever I may serve you,

T.M.

To whom the letter was written, or by whom, does not appear. The writer appears to have been of good position in Sir Thos. Fairfax's army; and it may have been Sir Richard Fortescue whom he addressed.

The taking of the frigate in Falmouth harbour is, with some additional particulars, mentioned, under date "Thursday, March the 19," in a newspaper headed "Perfect Occurrences of both Houses of Parliament, and Martiall Affairs." "We have taken a ship at Falmouth, that fought some houres; it is laden with wines, some letters are intercepted to the King, and others also from Ireland, (again). *Pendennis* not yet summoned, the Generall exceeding busie at Truro, *Hopton* not yet declared what he will do, very few go to the King."

In point of fact, Pendennis was summoned the day previous, namely the 18th. On that day, Sir Thos. Fairfax summoned Col. Arundel to surrender the castle of Pendennis on fitting conditions. His haughty letter is preserved, along with Col. Arundel's reply to it, amongst the Clarendon State Papers.

Sir Thomas Fairfax to Mr. John Arundel,

Sir,—Being come into these parts with the army, where it hath pleased God to give us so good success, as now no body of an army is remaining to oppose us, nor indeed through the great mercy of God in any part of the Kingdom considerable: I thought fit before any extremity of force were used against you, to send you this summons, by which I demand you to deliver up the Castle of Pendennis, and all things belonging to that Garrison for the service of the Kingdom, which if you incline to, you may have conditions befitting yourself and the quality of those that are with you: I expect your answer in two hours, and rest Your Servant,

THOMAS FAIRFAX.

The governor of Pendennis castle took "less than two minutes resolution," and returned immediately this spirited reply.

Col. John Arundel to Sir Thomas Fairfax,

Sir,—The Castle was committed to my Government by his Majesty, who by our laws hath the command of the Castles and Forts of this Kingdom; and my age of seventy summons me hence shortly. Yet I shall desire no other testimony to follow my departure than my conscience to God and loyalty to his Majesty, whereto I am bound by all the obligations of nature, duty, and oath. I wonder you demand the Castle without authority from his Majesty; which if I should render, I brand myself and my posterity with the indelible character of Treason. And having taken less than two minutes resolution, I resolve that I will here bury myself before I deliver up this Castle to such as fight against his Majesty, and that nothing you can threaten is formidable to me in respect of the loss of loyalty and conscience. Your Servant,

JOHN ARUNDEL, OF TRERISE.
18. March 1645.

Pendennis castle was invested closely by land and by sea. It held out gallantly for five months, from the middle of March until the middle of August, 1646, and was the last fortress but one, (Raglan castle, Monmouthshire), that surrendered to the parliament.

During the siege, little appears to have been done in the way of actual bombardment, though there are still shot marks on the north west side of the castle, from which it has been supposed that the garrison did suffer from bombardment to some extent. It suffered principally from want of provisions, and towards the end was reduced to a deplorable condition. However, when it became at length impossible to hold out any longer, and negotiations were entered into for the surrender, with such spirit on the part of the besieged were they carried on, that the real condition of the garrison was unsuspected by the other party, and as advantageous terms were procured for this as had been obtained by any other garrison during the war.

How much interest was felt by parliament and the nation in the siege, and how closely its progress was watched, is shown in the newspapers of the period.

The " Mercurius Britanicus" for the 16th to the 23rd March, 1646, gives the following " Intelligence. The *King's* Western Army quite moldered away : *Hopton*, *Capel*, and *Wentworth* bound for another Country. We have gained as great a power over the Harbour at *Falmouth*, as they in *Pendennis*, who will have enough to do now to preserve themselves." The fort of St. Mawes, it will be remembered, had surrendered to the parliament, on the 16th.

The "Weekly Account" for the 25th to the 31st of March, 1646, prints a letter dated "Bodman, March 24," which begins, "The Generall with the body of the Army is now come to Bodman, having left Colonell Hammon with a sufficient strength of Horse and Foot to block up Pendennis by Land, which will be easily done by raising Fortifications upon the Isthmus, which is very narrow."

The same newspaper contains intelligence for the 26th :—"This day came the unwelcome newes of the death of that religious and truly valiant Gentleman Colonel Ingoldsby who with other Commanders going to view Pendennis Castle received a shot from the Enemy who lay in ambush behind a Mud-wall."

The " Moderate Intelligencer" (no. 56), under date "Saturday, March 28." has this. " Letters from the west tell us, that his Excellency Sir *Tho. Fairfax* having left *Pendennis* almost lined about, and sent a party towards the Mount of countrymen to block it up, was returned to *Bodman* from *Truro*, which was 20 miles, and all in one day : As for the Mount, there is 700 men in it, yet its conceived not to be a long work. When col. *Hamond,* who as before we told you was before *Pendennis* castle, with col. *Ingoldsby,* and col. *Fortescues* Regiments, hath perfected the Line, and some *Cornish* are come to assist at *Pendennis,* he is to attempt upon the Mount :......as for *Pendennis,* they are blades of the right stamp, and having within 200 Tun of wine, spare not to be daily drunk, and this the Governour incourages, that their discontents take not overmuch hold of them, which are very great already, they are at sixpence *per diem*, nor will that hold long."

" Sir Ralph Hopton and Lord Capel embarked at Pendennis, and joined the Prince of Wales at Scilly, on April 11." (Life of Fairfax, p. 267).

On the 11th April, 1646, the Council of War at Pendennis castle, wrote a letter of intelligence and entreaty to the prince, informing him, that the quarters of the emeny, as to the land forces, were at Arwenack house, and they had a line from sea to sea ; that the garrison were in a bad state, and that there was great want of clothes : and praying, that supplies might be sent speedily from France and Ireland. The letter was signed by John Arundel and 21 others. (Clar. St. Pa., no. 2171). Enclosed in this letter, was a paper, showing the "provisions designed " for the garrison of Pendennis, for 1500 men, for 6 months, (the list ending with 20 gross of tobacco pipes), to be sent from Ireland. (No. 2195).

The "Scotch Dove" (no. 129), for the 8th to the 15th April, says :—" From *Pendennis* is certified that the line is nere perfected, and the Castle close blockt up ; the Enemy are full of jealousie one of another, many drop away and

ENTRANCE TO FALMOUTH HARBOUR.—FROM PENDENNIS.

come to us. Captaine *Rivers*, and a Lieutenant-Col. came out and brought 52 men with them."

With regard to the entrenchments of the blockading forces, it should here be mentioned that they extended close to Arwenack. Many of their works were conspicuous in 1824 (when Hitchins and Drew's history was published), stretching from the bottom of the Rope Walk behind Arwenack across the isthmus to the sea, and which must have cut off all communication between the garrison of Pendennis and the adjacent conntry.

On the part of the defenders, the brow of Pendennis hill was defended by a hornwork consisting of a pentagonal redoubt, with flanks " *en tenaille.*" The parapets and ditch of this redoubt still remain, though overgrown with bushes ; the flanking lines can barely be traced. Old Tilbury seems to have been a good engineer, judging from the judicious tracing of these works, which effectually command the isthmus.

On the 17th April, Colonel Arundel was a second time summoned to surrender Pendennis castle to the parliament. This time the summons was by a letter addressed to him by Col. Robert Hammond, who probably had been left by Sir Thomas Fairfax in command. Col. Hammond's letter is amongst the Clarendon State Papers, (no. 2183), but I find no copy of it in the British Museum.

To this letter, John Arundel returned answer the same day, that he had already answered Sir Thomas Fairfax's demand, and he refused to surrender the castle ; at the same time he thanked Col. Hammond for the civility of his letter, (no. 2184).

On the 19th April, John Arundel wrote a letter of intelligence to Mr. Edgeman, in which he mentioned, that 800 of the Plymouth forces were coming to besiege them, and said, that both Pendennis and the Mount must soon surrender. (no. 2188).

The "Perfect Diurnal" (no. 143), mentions, that on the 19th of April, Pendennis was upon treaty for surrender. (And see The Weekly Account, no. 17). At this time Col. Hammond was engaged in reducing St. Michael's Mount, and Col. Fortescue probably was in command of the land forces besieging Pendennis, and if Pendennis was actually on treaty, it was probably with him.

The "Mercurius Britanicus" (no. 128), gives this intelligence of the 27th April:—"The strong Castle of *Dunstar* is surrendered to Col. *Blake*, so that there is not a *spot* of *earth* in the *West* but what is the *Parliaments*, save *Pendennis*, which holds out with an *ambitious glory*, that they alone remain *unconquered*, and so will do as long as their canary lasts; yet this humour is but a flash, and will quickly over."

On the 30th April, Capt. Batten, who was the "vice-admiral of the parliament's navy, investing Pendennis," summoned the castle to surrender to the parliament. Whitelock gives the 22rd May as the date (p. 206); but this appears to be an error.

The "Perfect Diurnal" (no. 147) contains the following :—

"The Summons from Captaine *Batten* to *Pendennis* Castle.

"Sir,—That you have been already summoned by the commander in chiefe of the land forces, I am not ignorant of, and as I am sent hither for the blocking up of the castle by Sea, as the Land forces doth on shoare, I conceive it my duty likewise to doe the like ; I do therefore in the name of both the Honourable Houses of Parliament, demand your Castle and Garison to bee delivered unto mee, to bee put into such hands, as may keep it, for the use of the King and Parliament, which if you consent to, I shal promise to all those that are desirous to go for *Oxford* passage by Sea to *Weymouth*, and from thence safe conduct thither. And if there be any Gentleman that desires to go for *France*, safe passage thither in these ships under my command and those that will go home to their habitations, to passe quietly without molestation ; And shall likewise grant any other thing, that is safe or requisite for you to demand, or my selfe to grant, I do not heare mention, the great blessings wherewith God hath blest the endeavours of the Parliament Forces of late, both by Land and Sea, nor the unlikelinesse that you can be relieved either by Sea or Land, if there were means to do it, supposing most of those things are sufficiently known to you, all my ayme and endeavours are, that this poore nation may be settled in peace, and every man enjoy his own, and if you deny my demands, I am not out of my way, for heare (God willing) I intend to spend the summer, what ever I do in the winter. *Sir your answer to this is desired by your* FRIEND VVILL : BATTEN,

"*From on board His Majesty's Ship the St. Andrews, 30 Apr. 1646.*
"*To the Governour Officers and Souldiers of Pendennis Castle these.*"

Still the garrison held out, and no doubt John Arundel wrote a letter to Capt. Batten, distinctly refusing to surrender.

It was probably in the early part of May, that one of the besieged in Pendennis castle, who had a turn for verse-making, and some scholarly attainment, besides such soldierly and noble qualifications as were possessed by "one and all," or, let us say, by most of the unfortunate garrison, celebrated their loyalty and endurance, and sang the queenliness and excellence of Pendennis castle, in an ode, so quaint, and so interesting and curious, that it deserves to be rescued from oblivion. It was printed in London, in the latter part of the year 1646, in a pamphlet concerning the surrenders of Pendennis and Scillie. The printing appears to have been somewhat careless. For example, "enlips" is printed for "eclipse," "Rune" for "Ruine," "as" for "is," "*ipsum*" for "*ipsam*," "*perses*" for "*perstes.*" I will give the ode corrected as to these errors ; and, for the further convenience of the reader, somewhat modernized in respect of punctuation, apostrophes, and other matters. The heading of the ode is, "Verses made in Pendennis Castle when it was besieged by sea and land." It will be seen, that these verses describe Pendennis as a most faithful wife, as a very Queen Penelope, who, during the long absence of her royal husband, her Ulysses, who is the King of England, is beleaguered by importunate suitors, Fairfax, Hammond, Fortescue, and Batten, but resists them all.

> Lady *Penelope,* fair Queen, most chast,
> Pendennis, of all Royall Forts the last,
> The last, the only, Fort ne'er conquered was,
> Ne'er shall be ; who in constancy doth passe
>   The rest of all thy sisters, who to thee
>   (The eclipse of all thy kinde) but strumpets be :—
>
> Great *Fairfax,* sonne of Mars, Bellona's love,
> Whose victories she prizes highly, farre above
> Cæsar's, presents the Trophies and Renowne,
> Promising the Queen of Forts a Triple Crowne.
>   Scorne the high climbering Phaeton. Or let the Sunne
>   Thy husband be, or be, for aye, a Ruine.
>
> Brave Hamond coveteous is, but cannot speed.
> But Fortescue is harsh ; of him take heed,
> He that so dogged is, now he's a wooing ;
> His suit, once granted, will be thy undoing.
>   If now the man his humor cannot hide,
>   Wise *Abigail* his suite will not abide.

Batten in's floating Castle, Neptune like,
For love of thee his lofty sayles would strike,
Become thy Captaine, might it be his hap ;
Thou shouldst fall fast into faire Thetis' lap.
    Or, wert thou fain, for the Indies, to be sold,*
    He'd Danae's Bosome fill with showres of gold.

He'd court his Lady, like a silver swan
Vpon the mayne ; nor should there be a man
In's winged fleet, that should not speak thee faire,
But, with his cannon thunderings in the aire,
    Would make thee musick, and withall to wonder,
    To hear him speake so sweetly, and to thunder.

Weepe not as one forsaken and forlone ;
Thine own Vlysses will, in time, returne,
Embrace, and hugge, thee in his Royall Armes,
Ne'er conquered yet by force, nor woon by charmes.—
    Brave Governor, be still but what thou art,
    England may be subdued erse thy great heart.

The following note is appended to the verses :—

" The Author of these verses after the surrender added the ensuing:—

"OVID.   Penelopen ipsam, perstes modo, tempore vinces."

On the 21st May, Lord Jermyn wrote from St. Germains to Lord Culpeper, referring to letters he had received about Pendennis castle, and giving directions for its relief (Clar. St. Pa., no. 2224).

Polwhele says (Vol. 4, p. 101, note, citing Tonkin's MSS.), that "Lewis Tremayne of Heligan in St. Ewe, Lieutenant Colonel, was in the castle of Pendinas during the siege ; whence he made almost a miraculous escape by swimming over from one of the block-houses to Trefusis-point, through all the

---

* This line is conjectural. The pamphlet, which has several misprints elsewhere, certainly has some here. It gives the line thus :—Or, where they love forth Indies, to be sold.

enemy's fire." If this story is true, Lieut.-Col. Lewis Tremayne must be distinguished from Col. Lewis Tremayne, who was in the castle at the surrender.

Whitelock chronicles (p. 208) that "A ship was taken with Ammunition and
Provisions for Relief of *Pendennis* Castle, and divers letters intercepted in her."
June the 12th, 1646. And the "Perfect Diurnal" (no. 150) gives this intelli-
gence :—"The house this day received a Letter of the taking a Ship with
Ammunition, and Provision for reliefe of Pendennis Castle, and many Letters
therein from the Prince, M. *Hide* and others which was enclosed in the said
Letters. The house ordered, in respect the Letters were in ciphers, that they
should be referred to a C[ommittee] to finde out the keys to the ciphers."

The "Weekly Account" (no. 25), under date June 15, has this : "Letters
from our Leaugre before Pendennis in Cornwall intimates that the Enemy in
the Castle begins to droop, having received the unwelcom'd news of the
taking of their ship laden with Provisions and Ammunition intended for
reliefe of the said Castle, so that it is probable there will be capitulations suddenly, & great hopes of their surrendring."

On the 27th June, J. Digby and thirteen others in Pendennis castle, wrote
a letter to the prince, informing him that they were reduced to the last extremity, and must, if not relieved, surrender in three weeks. The copy of this
letter, which is among the Clarendon State Papers (no. 2251) is endorsed by
Lord Clarendon, "Received July 13, at Jersey, and sent at once to the
Prince."

"The Moderate Intelligencer" (no. 69), under date June 30, has this :—
"The letters from *Pendennis* say, the souldiers run out daily, which its possible
may be a benefit to the Castle : The common report of the souldiers that
come out, is, that it cannot hold out above three weeks, they shoot con-
tinually both canon and small shot, and yet few have been killed."

"The Perfect Diurnal" (no. 153,) under date 30 June, says :—"great
hopes there is that *Pendennis* will be surrendred within 3. weekes there provisions being well neare spent."

In Sprigge's "Anglia Rediviva," published in 1647 (pp. 302-3), I find the
following :—"About the latter end of *July* the Enemy made a sally by Botes
to fetch in reliefe, but were forced back with losse. About ten days before

which a Summons was sent them, but they in hope of Reliefe by Ships from Saint *Mallowes*, returned a deniall ; and after those Ships were by contrary windes beaten to *Morleys*, yet the Enemy persisted in his obstinacy, expecting a propitious blast to bring their Reliefe to them ; nor could the fate of *Oxford*, *Worcester* and *Litchfield* surrendred, comming to their eares, work them to any other resolution then to hold out, without his Majesties speciall Warrant to surrender, whom the Governour was very earnest to obtaine liberty to send unto ; or if not to the King, at lest to the Prince, and would faine have perswaded Colonel *Fortescue* to condiscend thereto, as but a common curtesie, but could not prevaile, he not understanding it so . . . by a Lieutenant of ours, whom Colonel *Fortescue* exchanged another of theirs for, he understood that a Shallop had gone forth about the 26 of *July* to the Prince his Highnesse, to certifie him of their condition, unable to hold out many days without Reliefe . . . Captaine *Batten* kept ten large Boats and Barges well manned, before the mouth of the Harbour every night, within command of the Castle, drawing them off in the morning : One morning when he was newly drawne off, a Shallop got in by stealth, which caused great triumph in the Castle ; but 'twas conceived (and Colonel *Fortescue* was so informed by good hands) that little Reliefe was in it, save a Hogs-head or two of Wine . . . Some Overtures were made to the Enemy within, to goe for *Flanders*, an Agent from the King of *Spaine* came for that purpose, desiring to speak with some of the Souldiers in the Castle, while some of ours should be by ; which being granted, he made an Overture to some Papist Officers of entertainment in the King of *Spaine's* service in *Flanders* ; they desired to be satisfied of the Agents authority, and to see the conditions ; which being readily condiscended unto and performed on the Agents part, they answered him, That at present they were engaged, but should they be once free, next to their present Master they would serve his Majesty of *Spaine* : This curtesie was taken well from Colonel *Fortescue* by the Enemy and the Agent ; and certainly anything belonging meerly to civility, without involving danger in its consequence, was never denied by him . . . . The Enemy in the Castle kept fires all night, for direction to any Reliefe that should make towards them. They were very prodigall of their powder, making two hundred great shot in the space of three dayes at our men, but without any great execution, only three of our men being slaine thereby : The Work of keeping them in so straitly from Reliefe, was very great, and was not performed without very hard duty to our Souldiers, the Enemy within being so numerous, which therefore redounds as much to the honour of the Besiegers : and Captaine *Batten* with his Ships by Sea was no lesse carefull and vigilant, though indeed he wanted Shallops and Pinaces for the service."

" The Moderate Intelligencer " (no. 75), under date Friday, Aug. 7, gives this news:—" The letters from *Pendennis* tell us, there hath come in another Shallop, since that mentioned last week, but in both its believed little of relief, and the rather, because the Governour sent last week a letter to Col. *Fortescue*, to know if he had power to treat with him, and that, the conditions agreed, whether he would, or could give warrant they be made good ? alleadging, it would be a dishonour to him to treat, and when agreed, to bee contradicted by another. Colonel *Fortescue* sent him word, he had power : The Governour took some two days time, whether they be in treaty is not known, some think he will suddenly, others, that this is but a complement. Captain *Batten* doth what he can to hinder, but he wants shallops and pinaces."

In the same pamphlet in which the ode is printed, which is given above, there is printed an order, which was issued by the governor, for killing horses for provisions for the garrison. This order, which is undated, is as follows :—

" It is ordered, and Col. Jenens Levi : [this must be a misprint, and Col. Charles Jennens and Capt. Lewis may have been intended,] General Buckly and Maior Brittayne are hereby desired and appointed to view all the horses within this Garrison, and that they take particular notice of all such horses as are fit to be killed for beefe, for provisions for the Garrison, and that they give an account of their doings herein to-morrow at two of the clock in the afternoon unto the Governour and Council.

"JOHN ARUNDELL, Governour of Pendennis."

" The Moderate Intelligencer " (no. 76), under date Aug. 13, has this :— " We told you last week, that the Governour of Pendennis had taken time to consider, having rid himself & the Castle of a Gentleman, who is escaped to France, whose influence hath hitherto kept off a Treaty, is now begun to treate, and we believe will suddenly accord." In the newspaper entitled "Perfect Occurrences &c.," under date August the 15th, there is this :—"This day by letters from before *Pendennis* Castle, we were acquainted that the Treaty (by reason the besieged stand upon so high termes) was broken off at present."

It appears by John Haslock's account of the surrender, which will be cited presently, that one Digbie, with a hundred or more of the gentry in the castle, upon the breaking off of the treaty, engaged themselves by oath, to blow up the castle, and then to fall upon the land forces of the parliament, if honourable terms of surrender should be refused to them. However, Col. Fortescue "contrived a way to bring on the treaty again, which took :" (see *post*) or as the newspaper entitled "Perfect Occurrences &c.," under date Aug. 17, has it, "From the West, the letters speak of Messengers sent out of *Pendennis* Castle againe to Collonel *Fortescue* to treate for the surrender thereof, and that they seeme to be more willing to hearken to termes than before." "The Moderate Intelligencer" (no. 77), under date Friday, Aug. 21, has this particular account : —"We had this day the conclusion from Pendennis Castle, which was thus : Monday the 10 the Commissioners of both sides met, the names of those for the Parliament were Col. *St. Aubin*, High sheriffe, Col. *Bennett*, Sir *Geo. Ayscue*, Col. *Herlin*, Lieut. col. *Fitch*, Lieut. col. *Townsend*, Serjeant major *Jennings*, captain *Mainard.* For the castle, Serjeant major *Shipman*, Col. *Rich. Arundel*, col. *Slaughter*, col. *Jennings*, col. *Tremain*, L. col. *Brocket*, *Joseph June* and *Nevil Bligh* Esq. They sate in consultation untill Wednesday noon, and then their Commissioners brake off in great discontent, and away : we might here give you the demands of each at that time, and how they differed, but that will be superfluous. Colonel *Fortescue* finding this unexpected rupture, contrived a way to bring on the treaty again, which took : thereupon they began again, Friday, the 14, and agreed all by the 15, towards night, save the time of surrender: the 16, they agreed to the articles, and signed them, which are as followeth." Then follow the articles. And then the writer proceeds, "This so good a work of gaining this place of so great consequence, as it speaks much to the praise of all therein intrusted, so in particular of Col. *Fortescue*, who no doubt will be rewarded with that trust, and made Governour thereof, he is an honest man, and for the Establishment."

The full text of the articles for the surrender is given in the "Moderate Intelligencer" (no. 77), in the "Perfect Diurnal" (no. 161), and in "Rushworth's Historical Collections" (pt. 4, vol. 1, pp. 295-7). Rushworth makes reference to the surrender, and adds the articles, as follows :—

"Much about the same time was *Pendennis* Castle surrender'd to the Parliament, being a very strong Place, situate in the utmost part of Cornwall, standing upon the Sea, and commanding in a great part the Harbour of *Falmouth*. It had been Garison'd for the King by the Honourable *John Arundel*, of *Trerise*, Esquire, and was beleaguer'd by part of *Fairfax's* Army, under the Command of Colonel *Fortescue* by Land, and by Capt. *Batten*, the Parliament's Vice-Admiral, by Sea: And after a considerable Siege, and gallant Resistance, was surrender'd on these Articles. *Pendennis-Castle surrender'd.*

"*Articles agreed on the* 16th of August, Anno. Dom. 1646, *between Sir* Abraham Shipman, *Lieut.-Col.* Richard Arundel, *Col.* William Slaughter, *Col.* Charles Jennings, *Col.* Lewis Tremain, Nevil Bligh, *and* Joseph June, Esq; *Lieut.-Col.* Anthony Brocket, *on the behalf of the Honourable* John Arundel of Trerise, *Esq; Governor of the Castle of* Pendennis, *of the one Party: And Col.* John St. Aubin, *Esq; High Sheriff of the County* of Cornwal, *Sir* John Ayscue, *Knt., Col.* Robert Bennet, *Lieut.-Col.* Edward Herle, *Lieut.-Col.* Tho. Fitch, *Lieut.-Col.* Richard Townsend, *Major* Thomas Jennings, *and Capt.* Walter Maynard, *on the behalf of the Honourable Col.* Richard Fortescue, *Commander in Chief under his Excellency Sir* Thomas Fairfax, *of all the Forces of Horse and Foot within the County of* Cornwal; *and the Honourable Capt.* William Batten, *Vice-Admiral and Commander in Chief of the whole Fleet employ'd for the service of King and Parliament, on the other Party.* *Articles for the Surrender of Pendennis Castle, August 16, 1646.*

1. THAT the Castle of *Pendennis*, with all Fortresses, Forts, Fortifications, thereunto belonging, the Ships and all other Vessels lying under the Castle, with the Furniture and Provisions unto them appertaining, all Ordnance

of all sorts, with their Equipage, and all Arms, Ammunition, Provisions, and all other Implements of War, Necessaries and Commodities of and belonging to the said Castle and Garrison (except what otherwise shall be disposed by these Articles), shall without any manner of diminution, spoil' or embezzlement, be deliver'd upon *Monday* the 17th day of this Instant *August*, at Two of the Clock in the Afternoon, into the Hands and Custody of the Two Commanders in Chief by Sea and Land respectively, or such person or persons as shall be by them appointed for receiving of the same. And that immediately, upon signing the said Articles, the said persons shall be admitted into the Castle, to see the just performance of the Premises, and Hostages given for the due observance of them.

2. That *John Arundel* of *Trerise*, Esq, Governor of the said Castle of *Pendennis*, with his family and Retinue, and all Officers and Soldiers of Horse and Foot, and all the Train of Artillery, and of the Ships, as well Reformado'd Officers as others; and all Gentlemen, Clergymen, and their Families and Servants, shall march out of the Castle of *Pendennis*, with their Horses, compleat Arms, and other Equipages, according to their present or past Commands and Qualities, with flying Colours, Trumpets sounding, Drums beating, Matches lighted at both ends, Bullets in their Mouths, and every Soldier Twelve Charges of Powder, with Bullets and Match proportionable, with all their own proper Goods, Bag and Baggage, with a safe convoy unto *Arwinch-Downs*. And because his Majesty hath neither Army nor Garison in *England* to our knowledge, they shall there lay down their Arms (saving their Swords) unless such who are Officers in Commission, who with their Servants are to retain their Arms according to their Qualities ; Country Gentlemen and their Servants their Swords, only Ensigns their Colours ; where such persons as Col. *Fortescue* shall appoint, are to receive them : And as many as desire it are to have Passes from the Commanders in Chief, to pass to their several Dwellings, or to such other places under the Power of the Parliament, or beyond the Seas, as they shall desire, and not be plunder'd, searched, or injur'd in their March, or after, they not doing anything to the prejudice of the Parliament's Affairs ; and no man to be prejudic'd for the giving any of the persons

comprized in the said Articles, Entertainment in their Houses : And that the old Garison-Soldiers who have Houses in the Castle, shall have 28 days after the Surrender, for the removing and disposing of their Goods.

3. That the Prince's Servants with their Arms, and all Commanders, Officers, Gentlemen, Ladies, Gentlewomen, Clergymen, and all others, with their Retinue, that desire it, shall have liberty to pass with their Bag and Baggage, and what else is allow'd in the Articles, beyond the Seas ; and to that purpose there shall be provided by the Vice-Admiral a sufficient Number of Navigable Vessels, with a Convoy for their safe Transporting from the Haven of *Falmouth*, within 28 Days after the Surrender of the said Castle, to be landed at St. *Maloes*, in *France ;* and in the mean time to be assigned Free Quarters at convenient Places by Col. *Fortescue*, Commander in Chief ; and during the said time, that they be not plunder'd or injur'd, they acting nothing prejudicial to the Parliament-Affairs.

4. That Col. *Wise*, and all Officers and Soldiers of his Regiment, or as many of them as desire it, be shipt in *Falmouth*-Harbour, in Vessels to be provided by the Vice-Admiral, and landed at *Swansey* in *Wales :* And that such as are of the County of *Cornwal*, be shipt and landed at *Looe ;* and those that be of *Devon*, to be landed at *Yalme ;* and all to be shipt with Bag and Baggage and such Arms as formerly allowed them, nor to be plunder'd nor injur'd in their Passage.

5. That whereas by reason of the long Siege of the Castle of *Pendennis*, many of the Officers and Soldiers of the said Garison are grown into great necessity of all such things as might enable them to march to their several dwellings, many sick and wounded ; and to the intent they may be supplied with Necessaries for their Accommodations within the time limited to them by these Articles, it is promised and consented unto by the Commissioners for the Leaguer, to and with the Commissioners for the Castle, That Five hundred Pounds *Sterling* shall be deliver'd into the hands of the Commissioners of the Castle, or any Three of them, at 8 of the Clock To-morrow morning at *Penrin*, to be distributed among the Officers and Soldiers aforesaid as they shall think fit ; and they are not to take any Free Quarter in their Marches.

6. That all Goods taken from any person for the accommodation of this Garison or any person therein, shall be restored to their proper Owners, or such as they shall appoint ; and all Goods now in the Castle that properly belong to any other persons, shall be restored to the Owners thereof : And if any person carry away any Goods not properly belonging unto him, and deny to deliver them upon demand, in presence of any Officer in Commission, he shall lose his Bag and Baggage, and have such Punishment as the now Governor of the Castle and the Commander in Chief, or any Two of them, shall think fit : But all Persons may retain whatsoever was taken from persons in Arms, as lawful Prize of War.

7. That the Governor, and all Field Officers, with their several Retinues, shall be allow'd Carriage by Sea and Land, to carry away their said Goods to any place within their Country.

8. That no Officer, Soldier, or other Person comprized within these Articles, shall be reproached, or have any disgraceful Words or Affronts offered, or be stopt, searched, plunder'd or injur'd in their Marches, Rendezvous, Quarters, Journeys, Places of Abode, or Passages by Sea or Land ; and if any such thing be done, Satisfaction to be made, according to the Judgment of any Two Commissioners or more, being of equal Number of each Party : Nor shall any of the Persons aforesaid be compell'd to take up Arms against the King, nor be imprison'd for any Cause of publick or private Concernment, during the space of 28 days after the Surrender of the said Castle ; nor for any Cause of Publick Concernment, for 28 days after the said 28 days are ended.

9. That if any Person within the Garison be sick or wounded, that they cannot take the benefit of the Articles at present, they shall have liberty to stay, and be provided for at convenient places until they recover, and then they shall have the fruit and benefit of these Articles.

10. That all Persons comprized in this Capitulation, shall enjoy their Estates, Real and Personal, they submitting to all Orders and Ordinances of Parliament, and shall fully enjoy the benefit of these Articles.

11. That all Prisoners of War of either side be set at liberty : and that liberty be given immediately after the Surrender of the said Castle, to the

Governor thereof, to give notice to their Friends of the Surrender of the said Castle ; and that no Vessel coming with Relief within Ten days after the Surrender, shall be made Prize.

12. That if any of these Articles shall in any Point be broke or violated by any person or persons in *Pendennis* or comprized within this Capitulation, the fault and punishment shall be upon them or him only who made the Breach or Violation, and shall not be imputed or charged on any other not assenting thereunto, or acting therein.

13. That all Persons comprized in these Articles, shall upon request have Certificates under the hands of the Commander in Chief respectively, That such persons were in the Castle at the time of the Surrender thereof, and were otherwise to have the benefit of these Articles.

14. That the Commanders in Chief respectively shall give Passes to one or two Messengers with their servants, not exceeding Six, to go to the King by Sea or Land, from the Governor, to give an Account to him of the Proceedings of this Treaty and Conclusion thereof; and to return and receive the benefit of these Articles.

15. That Commissioners be appointed on both sides for the performance of the Articles, and Places appointed for the Accommodation of Sick Men.

16. That Confirmation of all the precedent Articles shall be procured from the Parliament, or from his excellency Sir *Tho. Fairfax*, within Forty Days after the signing of these Articles."

The " Perfect Diurnal" (no. 162), under date Aug. 31, mentions letters "from Cap. *Batten*," and says :—" By these Letters we had also the particulars more fully of the enemies marching out of Pendennis, as follows, That the number of Souldiers that marched out were 800, who laid down their Arms halfe a mile from the Castle, and disbanded ; most of the Officers and Gentlemen intend to goe beyond Seas. In the Castle was six double barels of Powder, 37 single found presently, more heard of, 1100 round shot, 2500 weight of Match, 2000 weight of small shot, 1900 muskets, 95 pieces of canon, a murtherer, some pikes, and brown bils, 4 Knights, 8 Colonels, 6 Lieut.-Colonels, 6 Majors, 17 Captains, 17 Lieutenants, 21 Ensignes, 3 Quartermasters, 15 Officers of the Traine, 16 Gunners, the whole number above 1000. 200 sicke left behind, 200 women and children, their provisions remaining little and bad, their spirits and resolutions great and desperate. A hundred of them resolved, yea engaged themselves by Oath, whereof the L. *Digbies* brother was one to blow up the Castle and themselves, if they could not get honourable terms, which was grounded upon the dissolving the first treaty."

The newspaper " Perfect Occurrences of both Houses of Parliament and Martiall Affairs," under date Aug. 20, mentions the surrender of Pendennis, and adds,—" 40 great Pieces of *Ordnance* taken, one great ship that bore the Queen formerly between *France* and *England*, one Shallop, and some other Boates, store of Arms, but Provisions little, as you may understand by the former, 7 great peeces of ordnance in the ship, many peeces unmounted about the Castle." (And see Whitelock, pp. 220, 221). These pieces unmounted, together with the 40 great pieces, would make up probably the 95 reckoned by Capt. Batten.

According to Sprigge (p. 334), Pendennis castle yielded 17 Aug., 1646 ; 17 having been slain in the siege ; 94 guns, 860 arms taken by Col. Fortescue: the commanders of the enemy being Col. Arundel and Sir John Digby.

A letter from John Haslock, (" Chyrurgion to the Vice-Admirall Captain *Batten* in the St. Andrew,") printed, in 1646, in the pamphlet above referred to in which the ode is printed, gives " A true relation of the surrender of Pendennis." The letter (corrected as to a few misprints and matters of punctuation and the like), is as follows :—

"Loving Friend, The well wishes of a friend, besides this.—These may as well certifie you of our health, as of the surrender of *Pendennis* Castle to Colonell *Fortescue* and oure Commanders. The very truth is, they would not have yielded to the Colonell, but, to auoyde contention, the Admirall desired they would treaty with both : which treaty at first did not hold ; for they had no mind to the land forces, (neither valued them), as, in my hearing, the governor of the Castle told the Admirall. But, as sure as may be, at the breaking of the first treatie, they went into the Castle, and took an oath, (all the Gentrey), to split the ordnance, of which we have found fourscore and odd, and to blow up the Castle, and soe to fall upon the land forces, to live and die together. This you may verye credible reporte, for I have heard it from the mouths of the best of them, and *Sir Henry Kilegrew*, my patient, with home I was two howers before they surrender'd to us. But the prevention of this plot was by meanes of the Admirall. For he had soe wrought with some that came aboard, that he put all the Souldiers in a mutinie : and by this meanes, *Digbie* and his crew could not performe their bloody designe. And soe they come again to treate, and surrendered the 17. Day. There was (noe bread) nor drink, onely a litle water, nor meat, only a cask of horse salted, but pouder and shot enough. We had taken their best shallop from them, that no other durst venter to them. I believe there is betwixt 3 and 400 sicke left behind ; the rest are marcht to their homes, only some that are to be transported into France. Haste calls away, but I hope to prattle more with thee over a pipie shortly ; therefore, only remembering my love to father Hadley, master Warton, Brother Baker, and all the honest crew, I rest, your loving friend, *JOHN HASLOCK.*"

The date, apparently, is about 26 Aug., 1646. (See in the pamphlet itself, the preceding letter of the 25th, and its allusion to this one).

The above letter was, with other papers, "printed and published by the Originall copies, according to order of Parliament."

The same pamphlet contains "A list of the Officers and Souldiers belonging to Pendennis Castle at the surrender thereof," called on the title-page, "A List of the names of all the Colonels, Majors, Captaines, Lievtenants, and other Officers that were therein."

The list gives names of 11 "Collonels" (including "John Arundel Governor," Sir Abraham Shipman, Richard Arundel, William Slaughter, Charles Jennens, and Lewis Tremaine); 6 "Lieutenant Collonels," including Anthony Brockett; 7 "Majors"; 14 "Captains," including Joyne; 5 "Reformed Capt."; 11 (more) "Captains"; 29 Lieutenants: 7 "Ensignes"; 10 (more) "Ensignes"; 3 Quartermasters: "Of Common Souldiers, 732;" (inclusive apparently of 300 "gentlemen that had command in the castle," and of whom 7 are named, one of them Nevill Bligh); "Of the Councell of Warre," 3, all named; "Of the Train of Artillerie," 8, including a General, a Controller, a Commissary of the Magazine, his assistant, Quartermaster, Marshall of the Garrison, and Conductors, all named; Gunners, 26, including the Master-Gunner, and the Waggon-Master's Man, all named; "Chaplaines," 5, all named; "Chyrurgions," 3, all named.

The "Perfect Diurnal," (no. 160), under date Friday, Aug. 21, has this :— " This day came Letters to the House of the surrender of *Pendennis* Castle on Tuesday last the most impregnable strength in England." The articles were agreed on Sunday, the 16th.

Lord Clarendon has a passage which is worth quoting, in which he compares with the conduct of other garrisons, that of the garrison of Pendennis, and speaks of how much their exceptional courage and virtue did for the cause of the king. This is the passage (book x. pars. 72 and 73). "72. Whilst these disputes continued between the parliament and the Scots, concerning the king's person, the army proceeded with great success in reducing those garrisons which still continued in his majesty's obedience ; whereof though some surrendered more easily, and with less resistance than they might have made, satisfying themselves with the king's general order, and that there was no reasonable expectation of relief, and therefore it would not be amiss, by an early sub-mission, to obtain better conditions for themselves; yet others defended themselves with notable obstinacy to the last, to the great damage of the enemy, and to the detaining the army from uniting together; without which they could not pursue the great designs they had. And this was one of the reasons that made the treaty with the Scots depend so long, and that the presbyterians continued their authority and credit so long; and it was observed, that those garrisons which were maintained and defended with the greatest courage and virtue, in the end obtained as good and as honourable conditions as any of those who surrendered upon the first summons."

" 73. Which was the case of Pendennis-castle; which endured the longest siege, and held out the last of any fort or castle in England; and refused all summons; nor admitted any treaty, till all their provisions were so near con-sumed, that they had not victual left for four and twenty hours; and then they treated, and carried themselves in the treaty with that resolution and uncon-cernedness, that the enemy concluded that they were in no straits; and so gave them the conditions they proposed; which were as good as any garrison in England had accepted. This castle was defended by the governor thereof, John Arundel of Trerice in Cornwall, an old gentleman of near fourscore years of age, and of one of the best estates and interest in that county; who, with the assistance of his son, Richard Arundel (who was then a colonel in the army, and a stout and diligent officer, and was by the king after his return made a baron, lord Arundel of Trerice, in memory of his father's service, and his own eminent behaviour throughout the war), maintained and defended the same to the last extremity."

Hals' account of the conduct of this garrison during the siege is also interest-ing. Hals says (p. 130):—"Which gentleman (John Arundell) was by K. *Charles* made Governor of *Pendenis* Castle; during whose Command happen'd a tragical Siege thereof, by the Parl. Army under Col. *Fortescue*; wherein Besieged and Besiegers show'd unparallel'd Valour and Conduct for six Months Space; when at length it was surrender'd upon honourable Conditions; the Soldiers going forth with their Arms mounted and Colours flying, more con-

sum'd with Sickness and Famine within the Walls, than destroy'd by their
Enemies from without : Having been driven to that Extremity, that the
Governor, Soldiers, and many other Gentlemen, and Ladies therein, were
forced for some Time to eat Horse-Flesh, for Want of other Victuals; being
hemm'd in by the Parliament's frigats at Sea on one Side, and surrounded by
their Army at Land on t'other ; so that no Relief of Men or Provisions
could be brought into the Garrison. Whereby it was forced to capitulate and
surrender as aforesaid, 1647, (before which Time all other Castles in *England,*
except *Ragland* in *Wales,* were yielded up to the Parliament). And the
Hunger-starv'd Soldiers of *Pendenis,* who came out thence, regaling too freely
on Victuals and Drink, brought themselves into incurable Diseases, whereof
many died. So that here, as in many other Places, it was observed that more
Men and Women died by too often putting their Hands to their Mouths, than
by clapping their Hands to their Swords ; as the *Jews* did on surrender of
Jerusalem to the *Romans* after the Siege and Famine there."

On the 25th Aug. 1646, in the house of commons, letters, with the articles
of the surrender of Pendennis castle, and a particular of the ammunition and
other stores found in it, and a list of the officers and others in it who surrendered, were read: and Col. Richard Fortescue was nominated and approved
of to be governor of the castle, and a committee was appointed to consider
how he might be settled in the government, and to devise for an addition
to the ancient establishment. (Commons Journals, vol. 4, p. 651.)

The house also, on the same day, resolved, "that the sum of Threescore
Pounds be bestowed upon the three Messengers, that brought the News of
the Rendering of Pendennis Castle ; to each of them Twenty Pounds apiece ;
And that the Committee of the West do pay the said Twenty Pounds apiece
to each of them accordingly." (p. 652.)

The house also, on the same day, ordered, that Tuesday, the 22nd Sept.,
"be set apart for a day of Public Thanksgiving, for the great Mercy of God
to the Forces of the Parliament, in the Reducing of the several Garisons and
Castles of *Worcester, Wallingford, Ruthen, Ragland,* and *Pendennis.*" (p. 652.)

And on the 28th of August, the subject having been considered also by
the house of lords, the 8th of September for London, and the 22nd Septem-

ber for other places, were appointed days of public thanksgiving. The entry of the order in the Lords Journals (see vol. 8, p. 475) is as follows :—

" 1646.

" Die Veneris 28° Aug.

" ORDERED, by the Lords and Commons assembled in Parliament, That *Tuesday*, being the 8th day of *September*, now next coming, be set apart for a Day of Public Thanksgiving, within the cities of *London* and *West'r*, Lines of Communication, and Weekly Bills of Mortality, and Ten Miles about, for the great blessing of GOD upon the Forces of the Parliament, in the reducing of the several Castles and Garrisons of *Worcester*, *Wallingford*, *Ruthen*, *Ragland*, and *Pendennis*, and that the Lord Mayor of the City of *London* do take Care that the Ministers of the several Churches and Chapels within the City of *London* and Liberties thereof, may have timely Notice hereof.

" ORDERED by the Lords and Commons assembled in Parliament, That *Tuesday*, being the 22th Day of *September* now next coming, be set apart for a Day of Public Thanksgiving, to be observed and kept in all Churches and Chapels, in the several Counties, Cities, and Places, in the Kingdom of *England*, above Ten Miles distant from the City of *London*, for the great Mercy of GOD to the Forces of the Parliament, in the reducing of the several Garrisons and Castles of *Worcester*, *Wallingford*, *Ruthen*, *Ragland*, and *Pendennis;* and that the Members of this House, that serve for the said several Counties, Cities, and Places, do take Care that timely Notice hereof may be given to the respective Ministers within the Places aforesaid."

Several of the historians of Cornwall mention, that John Arundel was succeeded in the governorship of Pendennis castle by Col. Richard Fortescue. He it was to whom the castle had surrendered in August, 1646. In the Commons Journals (vol. 5, p. 110), is found this entry for the 12th March, 1647 :—" That this House doth allow of Col. *Richard Fortescue* to be Governor of *Pendennis Castle.*"

Col. Fortescue did not remain long in the enjoyment of the governorship. On the 17th April, 1648, the house of commons ordered the castle to be delivered up to Sir Hardres Waller : and "further *ordered*, that the Captain, Lieutenant, and Soldiers in the said Castle, upon the delivery up of the said

Castle, shall be indemnified in what they have formerly done." (Com. Jour. vol. 5, pp. 533-4.) What it was that they had formerly done, and were to be indemnified in, does not appear : neither does the reason of Col. Fortescue's being deprived of the captainship in favour of Sir Hardres Waller appear. Possibly the explanation might be found in a letter of intelligence, dated 17-20 April, which is amongst the Clarendon State Papers (no. 2764), and mentions that Sir H. Waller was repulsed by Fortescue of Pendennis. However, the orders of the commons were agreed to by the lords, the same 17th April. (see p. 534.)

The chaplain of Pendennis castle, under Sir Hardres Waller, was Mr. Henry Flamank. This reverend and honourable gentleman, it may here be mentioned, was, in 1662, "ejected" from the church of England and from the living of Lanivet, which he then held, by means of the Bartholomew Day Act of Uniformity ; which was the occasion upon which so many ministers of the church of England nobly relinquished their livings, as they could no longer, after the passing of that act, hold them, without violating their consciences. And a memorial of Mr. Henry Flamank is accordingly to be found in Calamy's Nonconformists' Memorial. Calamy says of him (vol. 1, p. 353);— " He was a very genteel man, of considerable learning, great natural abilities, a clear head, a strong memory, and lively affections. His method of preaching had in it something so peculiarly convincing, that it seldom failed of some success. Such a happy mixture of seriousness and good nature, is rarely to be met with, especially so recommended by those stated evidences of sincerity, which rendered him unsuspected of affectation or ill design. He was very much esteemed by the more serious gentry of the Western counties, and beloved as well as reverenced by meaner persons." Some considerable time after his expulsion from Lanivet, he was called to be minister to a congregation at Tavistock, where he died in 1693. (see Jour. Roy. Inst. Corn., for Oct., 1865, p. 74.)

According to Drew (Hitch. and Dr., vol. 2, p. 129), one Shrubsall was governor of Pendennis castle, during the Commonwealth. Certainly he was not governor. He may probably have been lieutenant-governor, under Sir Hardres Waller.

The Puritan soldiers of the castle, under Shrubsall, are said to have wantonly destroyed the remains of a desolated college at St. Buryan (p. 129.) Other ravages committed in the neighbourhood at this period, are also attributed to the soldiers of Pendennis castle ; for instance, the Logan stone of Mên-amber, in the parish of Crowan, is said to have been thrown off its balance, by a detachment sent from Pendennis for the purpose; a most improbable tradition. The insignia of royalty were mutilated in those times certainly, as well as anything that was thought to savour of image worship ; but even this, doubtless, was done only by the lower and baser description of fanatic troopers, and was discouraged by the higher-minded and better educated officers.

One of the King's Pamphlets, published in April, 1649, in London, is entitled, "A great fight near Pendennis Castle in Cornwall between the Lord Hopton and the Parliaments Forces, upon the landing of his men for the fetching in of provision." The account given of this "great fight" is as follows :—"The Lord *Hopton* struck in at a Creek near *Pendennis,* where he landed many of his men for the fetching in of provision, and other accommodation ; but before they could facilitate and accomplish their Design, the *Parliaments* Forces at *Pendennis* having notice thereof, a considerable party of Horse and Foot were forthwith commanded out, who hastned to welcome their coming in, and endeavoured to get between them and the water, for the intercepting of their passage ; but through the malignity of the Cornish men their design was almost frustrated ; for after few hours march they were discovered, and the Enemy in a posture to receive them, who upon their neer approach saluted each other with the tokens of *Mars,* and after a hot conflict the *Hoptonians* retreated within command of their Ships, our men pursued, kiled 19, wounded many, and made good their retreat with the losse of 7 men. Their ordnance did much retard our pursuit, by which meanes most of them got safe aboard having many Boats in readiness to receive them ; otherwise few of them had escaped : some of the Land souldiers deserted them at their coming ashore, who say, That the Lord *Hopton* is commander in chief of that Squadron, and of all the Land forces thereunto belonging, and that his Colours (or Ensigns) are yelow, with black bulets in the midst, and on the top thereof, this Motto written in Characters of Gold, *For Charles the Second.*" (p. 3.)

On the 28th March, 1650, the house of commons had the articles for the surrender of Pendennis castle in Aug. 1646, under consideration. They had not at that time been confirmed, nor were they then confirmed. (Com. Jour., vol. 6, p. 388).

On the 10th May, 1650, the commons ordered, that " each of the Four Foot Companies at *Pendennis Castle, Dennis Fort,* and the *Mount,* be completed to the Number of Sixscore ;" and that the committee of the army should pay them after they had been mustered, in like manner with the rest of the army. (Com. Jour., vol. 6, p. 411).

I find the following notice of the imprisonment of William Prynne in the castle, (communicated by Mr. William Sandys), in " Notes and Queries," 3rd ser., vol. 3, p. 392 :—" William Prynne was a prisoner in Pendennis castle in 1652 ; where, as he says, he had ' few books, and less light to read.' While there he ' penned' :—' Pendennis, and all other standing Forts, Dismantled ; or, Eight Military Aphorisms, Demonstrating the Uselessness, unprofitableness, hurtfulness, and Prodigall Expensiveness of all standing English Forts and Garrisons, to the People of England,' &c. Published, 1657. Amongst other examples of the uselessness, as he calls it, of garrisons or forts, he mentions that—' Since my imprisonment in *Pendennis Castle,* a Turkish man of Warr at mid-day, in the view of all the Garrison and my selfe, came up to the mouth of the Harbor, and very near the Block-house ; took a great English Lightor of thirty tun, sunk the vessel in the place, and carried away some twelve persons in it prisoners into *Sally* or *Tunis* ; after which she came close up to the harbour two or three mornings together, till chased away from thence by a Man of Warre.' This does not speak much for the gunnery practice of Pendennis at that time."

In Burton's Diary (vol. 3, p. 518), in a note, Mr. J. T. Rutt says of Sir Hardres Waller :—" He appears to have been in great favour with the Cromwells, and was as fully engaged as any of the High Court of Justice in the judgment on the King. Yet, on his arraignment in 1660, as may be seen in " The Trials of the Regicides," he prevailed to save a life, probably soon closed in prison, by professions of penitence which have been little credited either by royalists or republicans."

Whether Sir Hardres Waller was deprived of or resigned the governorship of Pendennis castle I have not ascertained. On the 6th Aug., 1658, the commissioners for nomination of commission officers had prepared a list of a governor and commission officers for the garrison of Pendennis, and this list was on that day reported to the house of commons and read. The list names Capt. John Fox as governor, and Robert Roberts as lieutenant. Whether Capt. Fox, as well as others in the list, was then nominated for appointment, or whether he was then already governor of the castle, appears uncertain. He is mentioned as governor of Pendennis in 1654, in the following, which Mr. W. F. Cornish, of Budock, has kindly copied for me from his books :—"Jane, the daughter of *John* Fox, then Governor of Pendenis, was born the 18th of february & baptized the 7th of March 1654." Not improbably he was lieut.-governor in 1654, and appointed governor, in accordance with a nomination by the commissioners, in 1658.

Lyson says (p. 105, citing, in note, "Perfect Diurnal," July 29, 1649) :— "After the surrender which took place in the month of August, 1646, the besieging officer, Colonel Fortescue, was made governor by the parliament : he was succeeded by Capt. Fox, and the latter, in 1649, by Sir Hardress Waller." But certainly, as we have seen, Sir Hardres Waller became governor next after Col. Fortescue, and Capt. Fox next after Sir Hardres Waller. Capt. Fox, however, may have been lieutenant-governor for years prior even to 1654. Robert Roberts probably was appointed lieutenant-governor in 1658.

On the 7th Jan., 1659, a letter from the governor of Pendennis castle was read in the house of commons, and referred to the council of state (Com. Jour., vol. 7, p. 805).

Whether the death of Capt. Fox occurred between this 7th Jan. and the 13th of February, 1659, I have not ascertained.

However, on the 13th of February, 1659, the house of commons resolved, "that Colonel *Anthony Rowse* be, and is hereby approved of to be, Governor of *Pendennis Castle.*" (Com. Journ., vol. 7, p. 842). Col. Rowse is not named by any of the Cornish historians in the list of governors. He probably retained the office until the Restoration, in 1660.

A curious verse, in which one Rouse is satirized, is cited by Hals. My reasons for thinking it not improbable that Colonel Anthony Rowse of Pendennis was really the person satirized by the Cavalier party in that verse, and that Hals was in error, in supposing that one Captain Rouse was ever governor of St. Mawes castle, will be found hereafter. The passage in Hals may perhaps not improperly be cited in this place. He writes (in Gilb., vol. 2, pp. 277-8) :—" During the interregnum of Cromwell, Sir Richard Vyvyan, as a person disaffected to his government, was displaced from the gubernation of this castle, and one Captain Rouse put in his place, which gentleman, as I have been informed, before the war broke out between King Charles I. and his Parliament, was of such low fortune in the world that he lived in a barn at Landrake, and lodged on straw, till he got a commission to be a Captain in the Parliament Army under the Earl of Essex, which brought him into money and credit ; so that at length he was posted the Commander or Governor of this Castle, who behaved himself so very proud, grand, severe, and magisterial towards the neighbouring gentlemen of the royal party, that it gave occasion to John Trefusis, Esq., to make this short description of him in verse, which the Cavalier party, when they met to drink the King's health, would commonly sing in derision of the Governor, and call it their passado, viz. :—

> In wealth Rouse abounds ;
> He keepeth his hounds,
> Full fourteen couple and more.
> When he lived in a house
> With a owl and a mouse,
> Oh ! they say he was wondrous poor.—Oh ! they say.

Part of this barn aforesaid, tempore William III, as I am informed, was converted to a dwelling-house, the other part was made a Presbyterian meeting-house, by Mr. Robert Rouse, of Wootten."

Chapter IV.

IN 1660, when all England was engaged in singing the favourite ditty,

> Oh the twenty-ninth of May,
> It was a glorious day,
> When the King did enjoy his own again,

on the restoration of Charles II, Sir Peter Killigrew was already governor of Pendennis castle. Lyson says (vol. 3, p. 105, citing, in note, "Mercurius Politicus," March 15, 1660); "In the month of March, 1660, Sir Peter Killigrew was made governor by General Monk."

It was of the Killigrew family, as we have seen, that the site of the castle was held by the crown. The house of commons, in 1647, had ordered, that Sir Peter Killigrew should be paid £2,000, in satisfaction for his services, and for his losses in connection with his interest in Pendennis castle. (Com. Jour., vol. 5, p. 19). In 1660, the yearly rent and fine under which the Pendennis lands were held by the crown, were, as we have seen (p. 10), commuted to a yearly rent of £200, with no fine.

During Cromwell's usurpation, Sir Peter, then Peter Killigrew, although of a family remarkable for their loyalty, contrived to make such interest with the existing government, as to procure considerable advantages for his town at Smithicke (Lyson, vol. 3, p. 100; Hitch. and Dr., vol. 1, p. 250).

" In 1660 a royal proclamation declared, that henceforward its name should be *Falmouth ;* and in 1661 it was invested by charter with all the dignities of a corporate town." (Murray, p. 401). According to Hitchins and Drew (vol. 1, p. 250), it was first named Falmouth on the 20th Aug., 1660. Lyson says (vol. 3, p. 100), " This town is first recorded by the name of Falmouth in the charter of King Charles II, bearing date 1661, which incorporates the principal inhabitants by the style of mayor, aldermen and burgesses." Amongst the State Papers is a grant, dated the 12th Aug., 1661, to the town of Falmouth, lately called Smithwick, and the port of Falmouth, of incorporation, with a saving of the rights of Sir Peter Killigrew. (St. Pa., vol. 40, no. 44).

State Papers issued at Whitehall, in 1660 (?), declare that five foot companies in the garrison of Pendennis castle are to be continued, under command of Col. Rich. Arundel. (St. Pa., vol. 26, nos. 16-19). On the 29th January, 1661, however, the king ordered the sheriffs of Cornwall to reduce two of the five foot companies of the garrison. (vol. 29, no. 63).

Not improbably Col. Rich. Arundel, who was the son of the Col. John Arundel by whom the castle had been defended against the parliament, and was himself in the castle during the siege, was in 1661, and during all Sir Peter Killigrew's government, lieutenant-governor of the castle.

On the 16th Aug., 1661, Lionel Gatford, D.D., petitioned the king for the vicarage of Plymouth, alleging, that he had served in the late wars as chaplain of Pendennis castle, to the loss of liberty and estate. (St. Pa., vol. 40, no. 57).

On the 31st Oct., 1661, a warrant was issued for Colonel Harvey to be sent [prisoner] to Pendennis castle. (vol. 43, no. 135).

A petition dated in 1662, of John Dewnes, for the office of page of the back stairs to the queen, sets forth, that he was twice in danger of hanging and twice of drowning, in conveying a letter from the late king to his majesty at Pendennis castle, within 12 hours after receipt whereof, his majesty left the country : that the petitioner was promised a reward, but never received it, and has been utterly undone by his loyalty. Annexed to the petition is a certificate of Henry Arundel and three others in favour of the petitioner. (vol. 55, no. 65).

Probably, Sir Peter Killigrew died, governor of Pendennis castle, about July, 1662. Col. Richard Arundel, the son of the former governor, Col. John Arundel, succeeded Sir Peter Killigrew.

The 29th July, 1662, is the date of a warrant to pay to Richard Arundel 2000*l.* at present, and such further sums as the treasurer shall find necessary for payment of the garrison of Pendennis. (St. Pa., docquet, vol. 57, no. 113). The 25th Aug., 1662, is the date of a warrant to pay to Richard Arundel, out of the revenues payable for the duchy and county of Cornwall, 377*l.* 10*s.* 8*d.* monthly, for the pay of three companies and three officers in Pendennis garrison. (vol. 58, no. 75). It is possible that Col. Rich. Arundel, at these dates, may still have been only lieutenant-governor.

However, in July, 1663, the lieutenant-governor was Col. Legg. Presumably therefore, Col. Arundel, at all events by that time, had been made governor. The 22nd July, 1663, is the date of a warrant to pay to Col. Legg, lieutenant of Pendennis castle, 1,143*l.* 11*s.* 10*d.*, for ammunition and provisions for the castle. (St. Pa., docquet, vol. 77, no. 30).

Col. Arundel is described expressly as governor of Pendennis, in a warrant, dated the 31st Aug., 1663, to pay him, from the revenues of the duchy, 377*l.* 10*s.* 8*d.* monthly, for the garrison, with arrears due since its reduction to three companies. (vol. 79, no. 111).

Amongst the State Papers, there are three several warrants, dated respectively the 22nd and 25th March, and the 2nd April, 1664, for a grant to Sir Nicholas Slanning, K.B., in reversion after Col. Rich. Arundel, of the office of governor or captain of Pendennis castle. ([Ent. Book 16, p. 74.] vol. 95, no. 11; vol. 95, no. 41; [Ent. Books 16, p. 122; and 21, p. 6.] vol. 96, no. 21).

On the 30th May, 1664, a warrant was issued to Col. Arundel to deliver to the ordnance officers 47 pieces of supernumerary ordnance unmounted, found in the castle in 1661, to be sent to the Tower. ([Ent. book 20, p. 16,] vol. 98, no. 133.) These must have been brought into the castle by Sir Ralph Hopton's infantry, on their retreating there in 1646, before the siege.

In 1664, that portion of Budock parish which lay within the fortifications of Pendennis, was cut off or detached from the remainder of that parish, by the formation of the parish of Falmouth, by Act of Parliament. (Hitch. and

Dr. vol. 1, pp. 251,5). It was deemed inexpedient to include Pendennis in the new parish of Falmouth, as it had been described hitherto in official documents as being in the parish of Budock. On this account it was retained as a portion of Budock parish, although detached.

Before the 18th November, 1665, Col. Richard had been created Lord Arundel. On that date, a warrant was issued to him by that name, to send 100 foot soldiers from Pendennis castle, with all expedition, to Plymouth ([Ent. book, 22, p. 311,] vol. 137, no. 36). On the 26th of the same month, Col. Henry Norwood wrote from Plymouth to Lord Arlington, that the governor of Pendennis was extremely startled by the proposition to send away 100 men, his garrison being only 200, and that he, Col. Norwood, thought the matter should be referred to the Earl of Bath, (vol. 137, no. 112). We may presume that this was done, and that the 100 soldiers were not sent away from Pendennis.

John Wildman was imprisoned in Pendennis castle in 1666. On the 12th January in that year, a warrant was to be issued to Lord Arundel, the governor, to receive into his custody in Pendennis castle, John Wildman, and to detain him prisoner there, for engaging in treasonable and seditious practices, ([Ent. book, 23, p. 5,] vol. 145, no. 4).

On the 26th June, 1666, Secretary Morice wrote from Whitehall, a circular letter to the governors of forts and garrisons, to the effect that, there being apprehensions of danger from sudden invasion, the king desired the governor to use all industry to have his works repaired, fortified, and victualled for two months, and to fill up the allotted number of soldiers. This letter was sent to the several governors of Portsmouth, Plymouth, Tynemouth, Dover, Hull, Pendennis, Berwick, Scarborough, Landguard Fort, Isle of Wight, and Holy Island, ([Ent. book, 14, pp. 98, 9], vol. 160, no. 5). On the 11th July, 1666, Francis Bellott wrote from Pendennis to Williamson, the editor of the Gazette, saying: Lord Arundel, the governor, has been to the castle, according to the king's commands, and has ordered provisions for the garrison; he has gone to Truro to meet the deputy lieutenants and justices; the country is in a good posture of defence, and they profess themselves ready to serve, which both horse and foot proved in a false alarm (vol. 162, no. 78). And in a letter of the 23rd, he added :—Lord Arundel and the other deputy lieutenants met at Bodmin, and so settled affairs, that on any invasion there will be a full and noble appearance (vol. 164, no. 71).

It was at about this time that Major General Desborough was to have been imprisoned in Pendennis castle. By mistake for him a Mr. Desborough was imprisoned there for three months. On the 11th August, 1666, his wife wrote to Lord Arlington, saying :—Lord Craven and Sir Richard Browne have informed her how much she and her husband are indebted for Lord Arlington's influence in the Council, though a clause in the order for her husband's release will render him always a suspicious person, unless his own faithfulness may be taken warrant for his good behaviour, he having ventured his life in His Majesty's service ; her husband has been prisoner three months in Pendennis castle, in mistake for Major General Desborough ; he begs consideration, his case being different from traitors and suspicious persons that go under bail ; his misfortunes have almost ruined him, being a younger brother, and his estate unable to bear the charges of imprisonment ; she begs employment for him ; he must remain where he is unless he can gain further liberty from the the council (vol. 167, no. 52).

It is probable that in Nov., 1666, Sir John Stevens was lieutenant governor of Pendennis castle. He is described in a letter of Fras. Bellott, dated the 21st Nov., 1666, at Pendennis, as governor of the castle, (vol. 178, no. 167). And it is certain that at that date Lord Arundel was the governor. The governor, however, was often absent from the castle, and the lieutenant governor, who usually resided there, may, very likely, have been regarded as practically more governor than the governor.

Consequent upon the great fire of London, and the Catholics being, "without shadow of proof," (Cal. St. Pa., Dom. Ser., 1665-6, Preface, by Green) fixed upon as the authors of it, the oaths of allegiance and supremacy were imposed in many garrisons. Thomas Holden wrote a series of three letters to James Hickes from Falmouth, in Dec., 1666, saying, in the first ;—the soldiers of Pendennis castle have, with one consent, taken the oaths of allegiance and supremacy, and received the sacrament : in the second ;—the only Pendennis soldier who refused the oath of allegiance and supremacy was one of Lord Arundel's own servants, a Roman Catholic; in the third;—the soldiers belonging to Pendennis have received 12 months' pay. (vol. 180, no. 25 ; vol. 181, no. 25 ; vol. 182, no. 4).

John Wildman, who, it will be remembered, was imprisoned in the castle in 1666, was set at liberty, by Lord Arundel, the governor, in Oct. 1667, upon instructions from secretary Morice. ([Ent. Book 28, p. 6.] vol. 219, no. 5).

The war with Holland being at an end, most of the soldiers of Pendennis castle were disbanded in Oct. 1667. On the 2nd of that month, Thomas Holden wrote to James Hickes, that all the soldiers in Pendennis castle, except 60 of Lord Arundel's company, were disbanded, and were to be paid off that week. (vol. 219, no. 25).

For the history of Pendennis castle, up to this date, I have been able to avail myself not only of the various Cornish and other histories, but also of the Calendar of State Papers. The Cornish histories supply little information relative to Pendennis castle after the year 1667. Of the State Papers of the domestic series, only those belonging to the years 1547—1639 and 1660 —1667 inclusive, are calendared. The calendar for those years appears to be very admirably done, and there is a good index to each of the 33 volumes. It may be hoped that many more such volumes will be added in due course. Meanwhile, the calendar failing along with the works of Cornish and other historians, I am unable to give the reader more than a very brief and meagre history of the castle from the year 1667.

According to Lyson, Richard Lord Arundel was succeeded by his son, John Lord Arundel in the governorship of Pendennis castle. I do not find any other authority for this statement. Lyson says, "After the restoration, Richard Lord Arundel (son of the brave veteran by whom the castle had been so ably defended), his son, John Lord Arundel, and John Grenville, Earl of Bath, were successively governors" (p. 105, citing in note Hals). But Hals's account of the governorship from 1647 to the Earl of Bath's time is as follows : —"After the surrender of this Castle, as aforesaid, by *John Arundell*, he was succeeded in that dignity by Col. *Fortescue :* and he was succeeded by Capt.

Fox. As after the Restoration of King CHARLES II. *Fox* was succeeded by *Richard* Lord *Arundell*, and he by the Earl of *Bath.*" (p. 130).

John, Earl of Bath, was governor not only of Pendennis castle, but at the same time also of Plymouth Citadel, From the following petition presented to him by Anne Pomeroy of Plymouth, and of which I have been furnished with a copy by the kindness of Mr. R. N. Worth, the talented and erudite author of the histories of Devonport and Plymouth, it would appear that Capt. William Pomeroy served the king in 1646, as captain of his majesty's ship St. George, which was intended or used for defence of Pendennis castle. This is the petition :—

"To the Right Honble. John Earll of Bathe,

The humble peticŏn of Anne Pomeroy of Plym? widd.

Humbly Sheweth

That Capt. William Pomeroy, Dec^d yor peticŏners late husband faithfully serued our late Soueraigne Lord King Charles the first of blessed memory in all ye trubles, as Capt of horse, against Plymouth, and afterward as Capt of his Maj^ts shipp' St. George, for defence of Pendennis Castle, & upon surrender thereof hee was forced to go for France, and from thence to Jerzie, where hee continued many yeares, and from thence beeing ordered & sent by his Majesty, our Soueraigne Lord King Charles ye Second to Scilly to conduct a ship frŏ thence to Jerzey for his Maj^ts. seruice hee was in his course thither taken & carried in to Plymouth, where hee was keept a long tyme prisoner.

Then upon his Maj^tis happy restoreation yor peticŏners sayd husband, was made Capt of his Maj^ts. Friggott Dolphin, in wch cŏmand hee dyed leaueing yor peticŏner five chilldren, and in a uerry poore and sad condicion.

The premises considered yor peticŏn^r. doth most humbly beeseech yor Lo^hp to recŏmend her distressed condicon to his Maj^ts Justices of the peace of the county of Deuon to the end, that at ye next meeting att ye sessions at Exon your peticŏn^r may receiue such reliefe for the support of her selfe and poore children, as is vsially allowed in such cases. And yor peticŏn^r shall euer pray for yor Lo^hp honnour and prossperitie."

The Earl of Bath wrote under the petition the following recommendations.

"Royal Citadell of Plym° Sep^t 22th, 1671.

I doe recomend the p'ticõn^r to his Maj^{ts} Justices of the peace and doe desire them, at ye next sessions for this County, to take ye peticõne^{rs} peticõn in to Consideracõn and to releiue her accordingly. I finding the Contents thereof to bee true.

BATHE."

The petition is endorsed,—"Mrs. Pomeroys peticon. To have 20 nobles as a gratuity."

In March, 1688, Sir Peter Killigrew, of whom the Pendennis lands were held by the crown, took violent measures for obtaining from the crown money for repair of the castle. Amongst the Treasury Papers, is a copy of a paper from Mr. John Kent, collector of the port of Penrhyn, touching £201 0s. 3d. taken from him by Sir Peter Killigrew, who came with an armed force to his house after 10 o'clock at night, Sir Peter saying, the king was his tenant, and Pendennis castle wanted repairing, and with the money he would repair it; and further touching the collector's arrest and confinement at the castle.

In 1689, in the house of John Waddon, who was then the deputy governor of Pendennis castle, John, Earl of Bath, the governor, "first treated with the Prince of Orange's Commissioners, in order to render into his [the Prince's] possession the castles of Pendennis and Plymouth, which soon after was performed, on condition of the Earl's holding his former dominion as governor of those places under him; whereupon he caused the Prince's declarations to be first proclaimed or published in those garrisons amongst the soldiers; who received and heard the same with great joy, shouts, and acclamations, to the utter destruction of King James's jurisdiction and power in Cornwall and Devon, and establishing that prince's." (Hals in Gilb., vol. 1, p. 105).

Hals (in Gilb., vol. 4, p. 116), mentions, that one Richard Trevanion, after accompanying William III, "in all his Irish and Flanders war," "was posted to the command of Pendennis Castle in Cornwall, where he died."

In November 1717, the castle was struck by lightning during a thunder storm. The lightning in its course struck through the walls of the building.

which are eight or nine feet thick, and it is said to have removed enormous stones of five or six hundredweight, and to have so damaged the fort, that for some time it was indefensible. (see Lyson, vol. 3, p. 104). This last word must be greatly in exaggeration of the fact : the portion of the castle struck may have been temporarily uninhabitable.

Hals (in Gilb. vol. 2, p. 278), says, "The Governor of Pendennis hath yearly from the Crown 182*l*. 10*s*. ; his Lieutenant-Governor, 73*l*. ; the Master Gunner, 36*l*. ; and two other Gunners, 36*l*. each." Hals wrote in about the year 1719.

I am indebted to the courtesy of the authorities at the war office, for the information, that Lieutenant Colonel Arthur Owen was governor of Pendennis castle, and that he died in 1774 ; also that Lieutenant Colonel Richard Bowles was appointed lieutenant governor in 1758, and died in 1769, and Colonel William Fawcett was appointed lieutenant governor in 1769 ; and Lieutenant Colonel Charles Beauclerk was appointed governor on the 16th Nov., 1774, and died in 1775 ; and Lieutenant General Robert Robinson was appointed governor on the 27th Sept., 1775. Grose names Major General Robinson as governor, as will be seen presently.

Col. Fawcett, the lieutenant governor of the castle, was appointed governor of Gravesend in about the year 1776. Major Newington Pool was appointed lieut.-governor of the castle, on the 2nd Oct., 1776. These facts, also, I have from the authorities at the war office.

Grose, in the first volume of his "Antiquities of England and Wales," published in 1787, in the article upon Pendennis castle, says :—"This fortress has lately undergone great repairs....Its establishment is a Governor at £300 0s. per ann. A Lieutenant Governor at £91 6s. per ann. The present Governor is Major General Robert Robinson. The Lieutenant Governor, Major Nevison Pool."

Lieutenant General Robinson died the 8th Feb. 1793 ; and General Felix Buckley was appointed governor of the castle on the 11th Feb. 1793 ; I have these facts also from the authorities at the war office. Lyson, writing in about 1814, says, (vol. 3, p. 105), "The present governor is General F. Buckley." And Drew, writing in about 1824, says the same. (vol. 2, p. 358).

In 1795, as I have said already (p. 10), the Pendennis lands were purchased by the crown, from the then representative of the Killigrew family, in fee, having previously been leased.

It was at about this time, in all probability, that Crab Quay battery and the Half Moon battery, were added to the fortifications of Pendennis.

Major Pool resigned the lieutenant governorship of the castle in 1797 : and on the 29th June, 1797, Capt. Philip Melvill was appointed lieutenant governor. I have these facts also from the authorities at the war office. Drew writes, (Hitch. and Dr. vol. 2, p. 256), concerning Pendennis castle, and lieutenant governor Melvill, (he was never governor). "On the south west side are several little dwellings, with beautiful gardens attached to each. These erections, and this cultivation, originated with Governor Melvill, who encouraged his soldiers to build cottages, and raise vegetables for their families, by furnishing them with tools, and with the ground on which these evidences of industry appear." The little dwellings and the gardens here spoken of have now been destroyed.

In the "Memoirs of Philip Melvill, Lieut. Gov. of Pendennis Castle; with an appendix containing extracts from his diaries and letters. Together with two letters and a sermon occasioned by his death. [1812] Lond.," mention is made of the care and interest he lavished upon the soldiers of his garrison, and it is mentioned (p. 117), that "Some French prisoners taken by our army at Corunna, and brought with them to Pendennis, were likewise the object of his care."

To lieut.-governor Melvill, Falmouth owes the foundation of the Misericordia society, and other excellent institutions.

Drew says of him, (vol. 2, pp. 257-8), "Among the brave defenders of this important fortress, the late Governor Melville, from the extraordinary sufferings which marked his life while in India, and from that humanity, benevolence, and piety, which distinguished his conduct while the commander of this place, demands a tribute of respect . . . . During his residence at Pendennis, he was respected and beloved by all who were favoured with his acquaintance. By his death the affluent lost an amiable companion, who was ever ready to stimulate them to every benevolent work ; and the poor, a benefactor who sympathised with them in their distresses." He died at Pendennis castle, the 29th Oct. 1811, (Memoirs, p. 153), and was buried in Falmouth Church. (p. 152).

In Falmouth church is the following inscription:—

"In memory of Philip Melvill, Esq., Lieut.-Governor of Pendennis Castle, who died on the 29th of October, 1811, aged 49 years. In him was united Exalted Piety, Unaffected Humility, Diffusive Benevolence, enriched with every grace that can adorn the Christian Character. He gloried only in the Cross of Christ."

Capt. James Considine was appointed lieutenant governor on the 2nd Nov. 1811; he died in 1814; Lieut.-Colonel William Fenwick was appointed lieutenant-governor on the 6th Jan. 1814: the governor, General Buckley died on the 14th Sept. 1823; General Sir M. Hunter, G.C.M.G., G.C.H., was appointed governor on the 22nd Sept. 1823: I have these facts also through the obligingness of the authorities at the war office.

Drew, writing in about 1824, says (Hitch. and Dr. vol. 2, p. 358), "Lieut. Col. W. Fenwick is lieutenant governor, and resides in the Castle." The Gentleman's Magazine (cii. pt. 2. p. 181, [1832,]) mentions, that Col. William Fenwick was "severely wounded at the Maya Pass in the Pyrenees, July 25, 1813; when he suffered amputation very high in the right thigh, and on his arrival in England was appointed Lieut.-Governor of Pendennis Castle :" and that he died of apoplexy, 7 July, 1832. The Bibliotheca Cornubiensis mentions, that he died at Pendennis castle.

General Sir M. Hunter was appointed to the command of Stirling castle on the 23rd July 1832; and on the same day General Paul Anderson, C.B., K.C., was appointed governor of Pendennis castle in his stead; Brevet Lieut.-Col. Loftus Gray was appointed lieutenant governor on the 25th July, 1832; he died the 20th Aug., 1835; and the office of lieutenant-governor of the castle was thereupon abolished : the governor, General Anderson was appointed colonel of the 78th regiment of foot, on the 9th Feb., 1837; and the office of governor of the castle was thereupon abolished :—I have these facts also through the obligingness of the authorities at the war office. At the present day, whoever happens to be the commanding officer of the royal artillery stationed at the castle, is the sole representative of the ancient governor or lieutenant-governor, inasmuch as he is the only officer in the place, as I happened to be in the year 1873.

ST. MAWES CASTLE.

St. MAWES CASTLE.

Chapter I.

N some ancient records, the village of St. Mawes is called St. Mary's *alias* St. Mawes, whence some have argued that Mawes is nothing more than a corruption of Mary (see Lyson, p. 153, and Hitchins and Drew, vol. 2, p. 348). Tonkin observes (in Carew, p. 337), that it was "called St. Mary's, for that it was built upon the priory lands of St. Anthony, a Cell of Plympton St. Mary's in Devon."

In 1542, Leland gives the name as S. Maws, S. Mauditus and S. Mausa *alias* La Vausa. He writes (vol 3, fol. 13), " From S. *Juste* Pille or Creke to S. *Mauditus* Creeke is a Mile *dim*. The Point of the Land betwixt S. *Just* Cr. and S. Maws is of sum caullid *Pendi*[*nas*], on this point stondith as yn the

Entery of S. *Maws* Creek, a Castelle or Forteres late begon by the King. This creke of S. *Maws* goith up a 2. Myles by Est North Est into the Land, and so far it ebbith and flowith ; and there is a Mylle dryven with a fresch Brook that resortith to the creke. Scant a quarter of a Mile from the Castel on the same side upper into the Land is a Praty Village or Fischar Town with a Pere caullid S. *Maws,* and there is a Chapelle of hym and his Chaire of Stone [a litle with]out and his Welle. They caulle this Sainct there S. *Mat...* he was a Bishop in Britain and paintid as a Schole-Master." And again (vol. vii, App. p. 121), " On the very North Shoore of the sayde Creeke toward the havyn's Mouth ys a poor Fischar Village cawled S. *Mausa* alias *La Vausa,* and nyght to this Village toward the same Haven ys a Fortelet lately buylded by the Contery for the Defens of the Haven."

" The name of this saint, says Mr. Whitaker, is so disfigured by provincial pronunciation, both in Bretagne and in Cornwall, that we should hardly recognize Maclovius in Machutus and Machu, if all the names were not used by the same author for the same person ; and should never believe St. Maudite, St. Mat, or St. Mawe of the island, to be the very Machu, Machutus, or Maclovius of the Continent, if the former had not been averred to have been what we know the latter was, a bishop in Bretagne. This stroke of traditional history rivets all the links of intelligence into one chain. The well, the chair, and the chapel, combine to mark the residence of the saint at this place. He came to Corsult in the Danmonian region, in that half of it which was then called Cornwall, and in that part of this half which was then denominated Corsult, but is now the parish of St. Just. In his way from Wales, he settled at a point of the sea shore here, then all solitary in itself, and merely a long sloping descent of rock to the water, with a broad, lofty heath at the back of it, I believe giving appellation to the whole. Here he lived as a hermit, forming himself a chair in the rock above the well, for enjoyment of the warm situation, in occasional surveys of the creek under him, of the harbour upon his right, and of the sea in front of the latter, then all assuredly as solitary almost as the very site itself. From this place, as the fame of his sanctity drew many persons to visit him, St. Mawes was induced to repair to the Continent, and he accordingly embarked for St. Maloes." (Hitchins and

Drew, vol. 2, pp. 349-50). These incidents are supposed to have taken place about the middle of the sixth century.

Norden speaks (p. 50) of "the castle of St. *Moze*" as being, with Pendennis castle, "a stronge defence of *Falmouth* hauen."

Lyson writes, (vol. 3, p. 153) "St. Mawes castle was built by King Henry the Eighth, for the protection of Falmouth harbour, in 1542." It appears however, from one of the inscriptions, which will presently be cited, that King Henry the Eighth in the 34th year of his reign, that is in 1543, caused the castle to be built. Probably, it was half built in 1542. At p. 99, of the Magna Britannia (vol. 3), there is a print of "Falmouth Haven, &c," from a chart drawn in the reign of King Henry VIII, preserved in the British Museum. In this print "Pendynas' is marked, but no fort is drawn there; St. Mawes is not named, but St. Mawes fort is drawn, and over it are written the words 'half made.' It would appear from this, that the building of St. Mawes castle was begun somewhat earlier than the building of Pendennis castle ; and the map may be presumed to have been made in 1542.

The cost of the building of St. Mawes castle has, by one of its lieutenant governors, been stated to have been "5000*l*. or thereabouts." (*Vide post p.* 87.)

The occasion of the building of St. Mawes and Pendennis castles, has been set forth in the former part of this work (p. 4).

Speaking of St. Mawes castle, Lyson says (vol. 3, p. 153), "Mr. Trefrey of Fowey, had the superintendence of the works, and at his request Leland wrote some Latin inscriptions, to be placed on the building." "And although (write Hitchins and Drew, vol. 2, p. 348), all the inscriptions that he wrote have not been engraven on the stones, the following still remain.

Over the arms of Henry VIII, as you enter, is

> Honora Henricum octavum Angliæ, Franciæ, et Hiberniæ, regem excellentissimum.
> Respect Henry VIII, the most renowned King of England, France, and Ireland.

Over the great door facing Pendennis Castle, is again the arms of Henry VIII, and on the doors are the following lines :

> Semper vivet anima regis Henrici octavi qui anno 34 sui regni hoc fecit fieri.
> May the soul of King Henry VIII. live for ever, who in the 34th year of his reign commanded this to be built.

On the front are cut the three following :

> Semper honos Henrice tuus laudesque manebunt,
> Henry thy honour and praises shall always remain.
> Gaudeat Edwardo nunc Duce Cornubia felix.
> May happy Cornwall now rejoice Edward being chief.
> Edwardus fama referat factisque parentem.
> May Edward resemble his father in deeds and reputation."

The first of these five Latin inscriptions, as Lyson mentions (vol. 3, p. 153), is "on the outside of the wall of the half-moon battery, in front of the Castle;" the second he describes as "over the front door, which faces the entrance of the harbour" (*vivet* should be *viuat*); the third, cut out upon one of the three barbacans, is seen when one has passed the drawbridge ; the fourth is about the southern barbacan erected by King Edward VI ; and the fifth is about the northern barbacan erected by him.

The third and fourth appear in Leland (vol. 3, fol. 46), in this form.

> Semper *Henrice,* honos tuus, laudesque manebunt.
> Gaudeat *Eduuardo* duce nunc *Cornubia* felix.

The first and second do not appear in Leland at all.   But Leland gives the two following, which do not appear inscribed upon the walls, or upon the bastions.

> Henricus Oct. Rex Angl. Franc. et Hiberniæ invictiss. me posuit præsidium reipubl. terrorem hostib.
> Imperio Henrici naves submittite vela.

Carew, in 1602, wrote (p. 337) ;—"Upon the east side of the haven's entrance, St. Mary's, alias S. Mawes Castle, with its point-blank ordnance, comptrolleth any shipping, that deserve a denial of admission or passage." And again (p. 362):—"S. Mawes lieth lower, and better to annoy shipping, but Pendennis standeth higher, and stronger to defend itself."   And Drew wrote, in 1824 (Hitch. and Dr., vol. 2, p. 348):—"This castle, though erected nearly at the same time that Pendennis was rendered formidable, and though built by the same monarch, is vastly inferior both in size and situation.   All the works of which it can boast, are completely commanded by some elevated ground close behind, on which none of the guns in the fortress can be brought to bear to dislodge an enemy.   The castle at present, though otherwise kept in excellent repair, is not fortified ; but there is an open battery below, near the edge of the water, which in conjunction with the opposite garrison, must very much annoy an invading foe."   And the Parochial History of Cornwall published by Lake in 1868 (vol. 2, p. 309), has the following;—" S. Mawes Castle, which consists of a round fort, and a battery mounted with heavy cannon, is in good condition, and effectually commands the entire entrance of Falmouth Harbour." The height of the building from its base to the coping on the parapet above the leads is 44 feet; but its extreme height, including that of the tower, is about 64 feet.

There is a tradition that King Henry VIII visited his two forts of S. Mawes and Pendennis. This tradition I have already noticed (p. 5), while treating of Pendennis castle.

The Latin verse in which Leland mentions St. Mawes and Pendennis castles, together with an English verse translation of it, will be found at p. 7.

CHAPTER II

ICHAEL VYVYAN, Esq., was the first captain or governor of St. Mawes castle.

Tonkin (in Carew, p. 337), says :—" The Castle was built and fortified by King Henry VIII, and upon the dissolution of the priory of Plympton St. Mary, the lands whereon it stands were given by that Prince to Michael Vivian, of Trelowarren, Esq., who was made the first governor thereof." But Hals (in Gilbert, vol. 2, p. 277), says :—" After the dissolution of the Priory of St. Anthony, 26, Henry VIII, 1535, this Castle and the land whereon it stands, together with the government thereof, as I am informed, was given by that King to Sir Robert Le Greice, Knight, an Arragonist or Spaniard, whose son, in Queen Elizabeth's reign, sold the inheritance thereof to Hanniball Vyvyan Esq. of Trelowarren, who therefore was made Governor thereof." Lyson (vol. 3, p. 154) and Drew (Hitch. and Dr. vol. 2, p. 349), leave it in doubt, whether Michael Vivian or Sir Robert Le Greice was the first captain. Hals wrote in about 1719. It is the fact, as will be seen, that a Sir Robert le Grys was, in 1632, governor of the castle. Of him neither Hals, nor any other of the above-named authorities, makes mention. It may, therefore, be concluded that the only governor with a name like Sir Robert le Greice, was, not the first, but the fourth governor. And Tonkin's statement may be credited, that the lands whereon the castle stands were given by King Henry VIII to Michael Vyvyan, Esq., and that he was made the first governor, about 1544.

The castle was strengthened and enlarged with two barbacans in the time of king Edward VI, it may be supposed about the year 1550. (See the petition of the lieut.-governor in 1631, *post* p 87.)

" Michael Vyvyan," the first captain, died in July, 1561. (See Calendar of St. Pa. Dom. Ser. Lemon, 1547-1580, p. 179.)

He was succeeded in the captainship of St. Mawes castle by his son (Hals in Gilb., vol. 3, p. 134), Hannibal Vyvyan, Esq., in 1561.

During his captainship, on the 12th June, 1577, an estimate of ordnance for the castle was made, which is preserved amongst the State Papers, (Dom. Ser. vol. 114, no. 13.)

On the 31st Oct., 1595, he wrote from the castle to Sir George Carew, lieutenant of ordnance, to the following effect :—I acknowledge the receipt of half a last of powder, and a ton of shot, return a brass cannon, a demi culverin, and other iron ordnance, as unserviceable, and want a receipt. I gave my opinion as to what pieces I thought necessary for St. Mawes' castle, where I will not dwell, unless I have a better supply, viz. a whole culverin, four demi culverins, and three sakers, with some more muskets and powder. (Vol. 254, no. 41.)

From an account dated the 23rd Mar., 1596, and preserved amongst the State Papers (vol. 261, no. 108), it appears that the captain's fees at this time were £118 12s. 6d. annually, that is, 10s. per diem.

If Carew's " general estimate " is to be credited, Hannibal Vyvyan, in 1602, had for St. Mawes one company of 100 men, of whom 40 were pike-men, 40 were armed with muskets, and 20 with calivers. (See p. 212.) I have already observed upon his general estimate.

Carew, after speaking of St. Mawes castle, says (p. 338), it " is commanded by Master Vivian, a gentleman, who through his worth deserveth, and with due care and judgment dischargeth, the martial and civil governments committed to his trust." Carew wrote in 1602.

Hannibal Vyvyan died, probably, in 1603.

He was succeeded in the captainship by his son (Hals in Gilb. vol. 3, p. 134), Francis, afterwards Sir Francis Vivian. Amongst the State Papers

([Ind. Wt. Book, p. 15] vol. 5, no. 1) is the grant, dated 1 Dec., 1603, to Francis Vivian, of the office of keeper of St. Mawes castle, for life.

During his captainship, on the 12th June, 1609, Sir William Godolphin and others wrote to Lord Salisbury, inclosing in their letter an estimate of expense of the reparations which they thought necessary for St. Mawes castle. (vol 45. no. 113.)

In 1623, Sir John Ogle and others were commissioned to survey the castle ; and they recommended, that £700 should be granted for its fortification, and that 10 pieces of ordnance should be allowed to it. (See the lieut.-governor's petition in 1631, *post*, p. 87.) In their report, they described the castle as of good strength and well situated, and out of reach of Pendennis shot, but overtopped with high ground. (St. Pa. Dom. Ser., vol. 186, no. 81.)

It does not appear that their recommendations were fully acted upon. However, a warrant appears to have been issued, on the 3rd July, 1628, for the payment of £253 to Sir Francis Vivian, for repairs and provisions for the castle. (vol. 109, no. 12.)

In 1630, Hannibal Bonithon was lieut.-governor of the castle, and had been probably for some years past. Sir William Killigrew, who, with his father, was then captain of Pendennis castle, in that year complained, that, for the last two years, ships had been stayed and questioned at St. Mawes castle, and this had been accustomed to be done at Pendennis castle only. On the 19th Jan. 1631, the master, wardens, and assistants of the Trinity House, on the entreaty of Hannibal Bonithon, certified to the lords of the Admiralty, that the castle of St. Mawes is of great consequence for the safety of the country, for other let to hinder the enemy from landing on the east side of "that port" there is none. (vol. 182, no. 75.) And on the 22nd of Jan. 1631, the mayor and burgesses of St. Mawes sent in their certificate to the lords of the Admiralty that the commanders of the castle there have required all shipping to make their repair to the castle for 40 years, and they have heard that the like course was used ever since the castle was finished. (vol. 183, no. 11.) And on the same day a similar certificate was sent in by the inhabitants of St. Just, Philleigh, and Anthony. (vol. 183, no. 12.)

On the 15th Feb. 1631, Lieut. Hannibal Bonithon, having drawn up an elaborate statement of certain chief points touching the difference between the castles, including some of particular interest with reference to the history of St. Mawes castle, embodied this statement in a petition to the lords of the Admiralty. The petition is amongst the State Papers (vol. 184, no. 22), and is worth giving *in extenso*.

> " To the right honoᵇˡᵉ the Lords Comʳˢ for the Nauie and Admᵗʸ of England.
>
> Certain cheife points considerable touching the difference now in question between his Maᵗˢ Castles of St. Mawes and Pendennys in Cornwall.

1. First that his Maᵗˢ Castle of St. Mawes in or about the 30th year of the raigne of King Henry the 8th was erected by the care of the State upon the east side of the mouth of the harbour of Falmouth for the better safeguard of the said harboʳ, and service of the said late King and his successors, and situate in the most convenient place for offence and defence to the purposes aforesaid costing his Maᵗʸ 5000*l.* or thereabouts.

2. It was much strengthened and enlarged wᵗʰ two Barbicans by the care of the King and State in the time of King Edw: 6, as a piece of principall importance fitt to be upheld continued and supplyed for his Maᵗˢ service.

And by both those Kings imbellisht wᵗʰ lasting ornamᵗˢ of their memory, wᶜʰ under favoʳ I believe noe fort in England hath the like, vizᵗ., having past the drawbridge, above his Maᵗˢ Armes stands cutt out in the wall, Semper honos Henrice tuus laudesque manebunt ; Round about a maine Bullwark oppositt to the Sea, intending a kingly cõmaund to all shipping, (wᶜʰ is now drawen in question) you may reade, Honora Henricum octavum Angliæ, Franciæ, et Hiberniæ Regem excellentissimum, within this foresaid work in the firme stony edifice is written, Viuat anima Regis Henrici octaui qui anno tricessimo sui Regni hoc fecit fieri.

About the Northern Barbican erected by King Edw. ´6, stands Edwardus fama referat factisque parentem. About the south Gaudeat Edwardo nunc Duce Cornubia fœlix.

3. The plott of St Mawes castle drawen by Mr. Norden upon special cõmaund in the time of Queen Eliz., wth a Blockhouse under it, no wais to be undervalued.

4. A draught of the river of Falmouth wth the depths at a lowe water, by wch may be seene the importance of St. Mawes castle, being opposed to the principall resistance of all Sea forces.

5. That in the time of R. Elizabeth, it was many times thought fitt to have been fortified round, as appeth by sundry plotts to that purpose, And some 7 years sithence or thereabouts, being viewed by his Ma^{ts} Com^{rs}, Sr John Ogle & others, recomended, and allowances for the fortificacon, and supply of it graunted, vizt tenn peeces of Ordinance, with 700*l.* or thereabouts for fortificacon, wch notwthstanding the present Captain thereof Sr Francis Vivian hauing many times petitioned for, and not gotten, yet by his own care and purse hath remedied many defects.

6. By the care and foresight of the now Lord Threr, [*i.e.* Treasurer,] it hath been of late within this 6 months or thereabouts exactly viewed by certaine gentlemen designed thereto by his lo^p, whose certificate will testify the useful necessity and importance of the place, and wch allowances is heere humbly againe desired may with fitt conveniency be dispatched.

7. That St. Mawes castle was erected before Pendennys or neere about the same tyme ; and hath been allwaise cõmaunded by two distinct, & not one subordinat Cap^{tn} to the other, but both imediat from the Kings and Queenes of England ; And the cõmaund of the said castle wth all the powers priviledges preheminences and regards thereunto belonging is graunted by Lr̃es Patents of his late Ma^{t}y to Sr Francis Vivian and elder then Sr Robert Killigrewes Patent, wherein yor Lo^{ps} shall fynd that Sr Robert Killigrew is to take noe other priviledge in that harbor for cõmaund then Sr Francis Vivian, or from Sr Francis Vivian.

8. That the Cap^{tn} of the said Castle of St. Mawes, & his Lieftenants for the tyme being ever since the erection thereof, haue used to cause all shipps passing or endeavouring to passe before the same into or out of the said harbour to strike their flags and to doe their duty to the said Castle, as to a fort of the Kings, and to cõmaund and cause the Cap^{tn} or Master of every

such shipp to come a shore to the said Castle there to be examined for discovery of such matters as might be for the service of the king and safety of the said Castle, without giving any unnecessary molestacon to the pties (wch they never haue donne, though it may be untruely suggested) The doing hereof hath been, and is a matter of due hono^r & necessary use to and for his Ma.^ty and his service in those parts, and the abolishing of it may produce very ill and contrary effects, whereof the dangers that may ensue are such and the like

1. St. Mawes hauing not the power to call shipping, her ordinance for the most part lying without, may be turned upon the Castle, or nayled upp.

2. The necessary use of her erection is taken away, being for the East part of Cornewall the principall defence The towne of St Mawes hauing been twice fyred, and the country thereabouts foraged by the French in the tyme of King Henry the 8.

3. Pyratts, and any enemy may enter that harbo^r, and runne wth in the Castles, where they may doe any spoile, ransack his Ma^ts. subiects, robb the Tinn Merch^ts, wch most consists in that port, and returne in spight of Pendennys, as it apped by Moy Lambert the Dutch Admirall, who received from Pendennys 27 shott to noe purpose.

4. Shipps in like manner wth prohibited goods, others also refusing to pay the King's Customs may pass forth, nay this will be noe sooner bruited, but you will haue the customers themselves carried away, when they shall heare St. Mawes Castle must not stop them, as lately they haue been threatned.

5. The principall bent of both those Castles is to keepe the enemy from coming in, wch Queene Eliz: was well informed of, Sr Nicholas Parker hauing procured from the Councill Board a warrant to fetch some peeces from S Mawes, she herself not only countermanded this warr^t but sent more peices thither.

6. Lastly the ill consequence, the like cõmaund being never heretofore sought by any, that two such absolute Forts, the whole strength of a Country should be reposed in one man's trust, expressely contrary to the gracious intentions of soe many famous Kings and Queenes of England as appeth by their broad seals.

Theis things considered, wch in his Ma^ts behalfe and for his service, I humbly present to yor Lo^ps ; May it please yor hono^rs that the premises may be seriously examined, to settle and confirme yor pet^r & his Successors in the due hono^r and exercise of the necessary and accustomed service aforesaid rightfully belonging to his place And to tak such further order touching the premises as to hono^r, state, and Justice shall appteyne.

And yor pet^r shall ever pray for yor hono^rs "

The paragraph numbered 7 in the petition, requires some little explanation. It will be remembered, that Sir Nicholas Parker, captain of Pendennis castle, was, in 1598, by letter of the queen Elizabeth, empowered to exercise the charge of captain of that fort by deputy, in case of necessity ; and subsequently, in exercise of the power conferred upon him by that letter, he appointed Nicholas Burton his deputy. Such a power was never conferred upon any captain of St. Mawes castle, and its lieutenants were appointed immediately by the crown. The captain and deputy captain of that castle, are curiously called by Bonithon, two distinct, and not one subordinate captain to the other, but both immediate from the kings and queens of England. He considered his own appointment, as being immediate from the crown, in that quality superior to the appointment of any deputy captain of Pendennis castle ; and it is to this superiority that he points in the curious passage I am noticing.

The petition was presented in February. In May, the lords of the Admiralty having heard both sides, ordered, that Pendennis castle was to call to account ships which anchored on the west side, and St. Mawes castle those which anchored on the east side of the Black Rock. In July, Sir William Killigrew of Pendennis, petitioned the king for that order to be stayed ; and the king, declaring his intention to hear the differences himself, directed the execution of the order to be stayed in the meantime : but whether he did ever hear the differences himself, is, to say the least, doubtful.

On the 16th Nov. 1632, in a suit instituted in the court of Star Chamber, by Hugh Trevanion *versus* Sir Francis Vivian, Hannibal Bonithon, John

ENTRANCE TO FALMOUTH HARBOUR.—FROM THE BATTERY, ST. MAWES.

Wilkinson and Henry Teage, the defendant Vivian, being captain of the castle of St. Mawes, was declared by the court to have practised a variety of deceptions in reference to his office, particularly his not keeping the proper number of soldiers in garrison, and his putting the money received for their wages into his own purse. He was sentenced to be committed to the Fleet, to pay a fine of £2000 to the king, and to be removed from his office of captain. As against the other defendants, the suit was dismissed. (Vol. 225. no 36.) It appears, however, from an account, dated the 13th Feb. 1633, of fines imposed in the Star Chamber, with marginal notes, that Sir Francis Vyvyan's fine of 2000*l*, for misconduct as captain of St. Mawes, was respited. (vol. 232. no. 43.)

—

N the removal of Sir Francis Vyvyan, in November 1632, from his office of captain of St. Mawes castle, Sir Robert le Grys was appointed to the captainship in his stead.

Certain notes made, on the 17th April 1633, by Lord Cottington, of charges againgt Sir Robert le Grys as captain of St. Mawes castle, and his answers to the charges, are preserved at the Record Office. (St. Pa. Dom Ser. vol. 227. no, 8.).

In 1634, Sir Robert Le Grys took it upon himself to displace Capt. Hannibal Bonithon, and to appoint John Stanbury to the lieutenant-governorship of the castle in his stead. Capt. Bonithon, however, made his case known to the lords of the Admiralty, and they took it upon themselves to appoint him to be continued in the office of lieutenant-governor. And on the 3rd of July, they directed Sir William Courtenay, John Trefusis, Richard Erisey and Hugh Boscawen to survey the ordnance and stores of the castle, and to deliver them to Capt. Bonithon, and to cause John Stanbury to surrender to him the keys and charge of the castle. (vol. 271. no. 10). And Capt. Bonithon thereupon was re-established in the lieutenant-governorship, of which he had never properly been deprived. (*vide super*, p. 90.)

On the 14th of August, the commissioners, having surveyed the castle, reported to the lords of the Admiralty, that they estimated the cost of necessary repairs at 534*l*. 10*s*. (vol. 273. no. 43.)

On the 19th of September, Capt. Bonithon wrote from the castle, to the lords of the Admiralty, and gave them a list of officers and soldiers within the castle,

there attending on the 5th August 1634. There were a master gunner and 12
soldiers. (vol. 274. no. 28.) And on the 28th of October, he wrote from the
castle to Lord Cottington, and enclosed in his letter a certificate of payment
to the porter and gunner of the castle, 12*d*. per diem, and every soldier 8*d*.
per diem. (vol. 276. no. 38, 1.)

Sir Robert le Grys, was succeeded in the captainship, in the year 1635, by
Thomas Howard, Earl of Arundel and Surrey. The 23rd of March, 1635, is
the date of the grant to the earl of the office of captain of the castle, "the
same being void by the death of Sir Francis Vivian, late Captain thereof."
([Docquet], vol. 316, no. 102). Sir Francis Vyvyan had, as has been seen,
been removed from the office, by the Star Chamber, in 1632, and succeeded
in it by Sir Robert le Grys. Although the death of Sir Francis may have
happened only a short time previous to the appointment of the earl, it is
rather unaccountable that the death of Sir Francis should be mentioned in the
grant to the earl, as making the office void in 1635. I do not find that the
earl is named in the list of captains of the castle by any of the historians of
Cornwall.

Capt. Hannibal Bonithon remained lieutenant of the castle during the
earl's captainship. In September, 1635, complaints having been against him
by soldiers of the castle, Capt. Bonithon wrote to the council, defending
himself with reference to those charges. (vol. 298, no. 33).

In the year 1636. a report was made on St. Mawes castle; it is a short one,
and it may be worth while to give it *in extenso*. It is amongst the State
Papers (Dom. Ser., vol. 340, no. 40).
"St. Mawes Castle.

Institution and Consequence of this Castle, vizt.

	p. Annum.		
	£	s.	d.
Earle of Arundel and Surrey Captaine at 3^s. p diem	54	15	00
The lieutenant at xviii^d. p diem	27	07	06
Fourteen Soldiers and Gunners whereof two at 12^d. p diem } apeece and ye rest at 8^d p diem apeece ... ... }	182	10	00
Total ... £264	12	06	

This hath allways beene paid out of his Ma^{ts} Revenews of Devonsheire and Cornwall.

There is a Company of 100 men neere adioyning that are appointed to address themselves to ye Castle uppon any occasion."

On the death of the earl, Captain, now Major, Bonithon, who had been, since 1630, lieutenant of the castle, was advanced to be its keeper or captain.

Not long after his appointment, namely in November, 1643, several soldiers of the garrison gave information against him at Bodmin, touching his conduct as governor. And in January, 1644, articles were exhibited at the general sessions of the peace at Truro, charging Major Bonithon with embezzling the soldiers' pay, smuggling tobacco, and disaffection to the king's cause. Subsequently, witnesses were called up and examined touching these articles, and their depositions, made the 15th September, 1645, are preserved amongst the Clarendon State Papers. The next day, Sir Richard Grenville wrote from Truro to the prince of Wales, and he enclosed these depositions. (Clar. St. Pa., no. 1961). It appears certain that the governor at this time was, even in high quarters, under suspicion of treason or disaffection to the king's cause.

Such a suspicion may be thought to have been justified by subsequent events. Not only did Major Bonithon, immediately after the treaty of Tressillan Bridge, send to Sir Thos. Fairfax to be received into favour by him, and offering to deliver up the castle, but when Col. Arundel, the governor of Pendennis castle, knowing the comparative weakness of St. Mawes, thereupon sent to Major Bonithon, inviting him to come in to the castle of Pendennis and join his fortunes to those of the true-hearted royalist gentlemen who were in garrison there, Major Bonithon refused this invitation, and chose rather to seek favour with the Parliamentary party.

Sir Thomas Fairfax, in his letter dated March, 1646, "to the Honourable William Lenthall, Esquire, Speaker of the Honourable House of Commons," in which he informs the speaker of the conclusion of the treaty at Tressilian Bridge with Sir Ralph Hopton, for the disbandment of his cavalry, to the number of four or five thousand, says, after informing him of the treaty :—

" The reputation of this hath already produced a surrender of Saint Mawes Castle, wherein we found about thirteen Guns, and a good proportion of Ammunition; which place gives you a better interest in Falmouth harbour, then the Enemy hath: For by the advantage hereof, you may bring in Shipping without hazard, which they cannot."

The whole letter is given in The Parochial History of Cornwall (Lake's), vol. 1, p. 155.

Another letter must be cited, which is of considerable interest. It is one of several come " to the House of the progresse of affairs in the West ;" and it had reached the house of Commons on the 19th of March. It is printed in the " Perfect Diurnall" for the 16th to the 23rd of March, 1646, and contains the following :—

" Every houre more Gentlemen of Quality doe come in, and this day Col. *Trevanion* came from *Penrin,* and some of his Officers came to *Truro* with their Colours flying, and their men armed even from the Lord *Hoptons* head quarters which are now at *Camborne;* This hath wrought such operation upon the Governour at Saint *Mawes* (the principall Fort that commands the Haven at *Falmouth,* having a greater command thereof than the Castle and Fort of *Pendennis*) that he hath sent to the Generall to bee received into favour, and will deliver up the Castle, Fort, Ordnance, Armes, and Ammunition: and accordingly there is forces sent away this night to take possession thereof. *Arundell* the Governour of *Pendennis* sent to tempt the Governour at St. *Mawes* to come in the Castle of *Pendennis;* hee refused the same and as aforesaid craved the ayd of this Army. There are two great Brasse pieces of Ordnance in the Fort, of about 4000 weight a piece."

Sprigge, in his " Anglia Rediviva " (p. 215), says :—Although *Arundell* the governour of *Pendennis,* sent to command him to come into the Castle of *Pendennis,* he fearing some evill intended against him, refused and persisted in his former desire : whereupon the General sent him conditions, with a Summons ; which were accepted, and he agreed to surrender."

And Sprigge mentions (p. 334), that the castle yielded on the 13th of March ; and that 12 guns, 160 arms, and 2 colours were taken by General Fairfax.

The castle having been surrendered to the parliament by Major Bonithon in March, was without a governor or a lieutenant-governor, until August 1646. On the 28th of August, Lieutenant-Colonel George Kekewich was appointed captain of the castle by the parliament.

The Lords Journals (vol. 8. p. 465.), contain the following entry for the 18th August, 1646.

"Upon reading the Petition of Lieutenant-Colonel *George Kekewich*: shewing, "That he hath been in the service of the State, in *Plymouth, Cornwall,* and *Devonshire,* ever since the beginning of these Troubles ; and being reduced, he is out of any Employment : therefore desireth some Place, whereby he may do the State further Service." It is ORDERED, That this House thinks it fit the Petitioner be made Governor of *St. Mawes Castle* in *Cornwall;* and that the Concurrence of the House of Commons be desired herein."

And there is the following entry (p. 475) for the 28th August.

"ORDERED by the Lords and Commons in Parliament assembled, That Lieutenant *George Kekewich* be Captain of *St. Mawes Castle,* in the County of *Cornwall.*"

A curious mistake appears to have been made by Hals, who believed that Captain Rouse, "during the interregnum of Cornwall," was appointed to "the gubernation of this Castle." (Hals in Gilbert, vol. 2. p. 277.) It is the fact, that one Colonel Rowse was appointed governor of Pendennis castle by the parliament in 1659. One may the more easily believe, that it was this Colonel Rowse of Pendennis, who was satirized by the cavalier party, in the verse which Hals cites, and that Hals was misinformed as to the castle which he was appointed to govern, when one finds that Hals was certainly in error in sup- posing that Sir Richard Vyvyan was governor of St. Mawes castle during the interregnum, and that Hals writes :—" During the interregnum of Cromwell, Sir Richard Vyvyan, as a person disaffected to his government, was displaced from the gubernation of this Castle, and one Captain Rouse put in his place." (p. 277.) Otherwise, one might have supposed, that during the governorship of Lieut-Colonel Kekewich, one Captain Rouse was lieut-governor of St. Mawes castle, and Hals' error was no greater than the common inaccuracy of calling a lieut-governor, governor ; and that it was by a curious coincidence, that during Capt. Rouse's lieut-governorship of St. Mawes castle, Col. Rowse was governor of Pendennis castle. Lyson follows Hals in his account of the governorship of St. Mawes at this period. (vol. 3, p. 154.) The passage in Hals will be found cited, *super* p. 67.

In 1660, shortly after the Restoration, Sir Richard Vyvyan, son of the former governor, Sir Francis Vyvyan, (Hals, in Gilb. vol. 3, p. 134,) and a zealous royalist, was captain of the castle.

It is of course certain, that so good a royalist was not appointed by the parliament, and therefore the presumption is, that Lieut-Colonel Kekewich, whom the parliament did appoint in Aug. 1646, remained the governor of the castle until the Restoration, and then was displaced in favour of Sir Richard Vyvyan, by King Charles II.

Among the state papers is a petition of "Sir Richard Vyvyan, Bart., Captain of St. Mawes castle," dated 1660. (November?). (vol. 22, no 192.) Sir Richard prays for a few more soldiers to maintain the watch ; he sets forth that there are at present but one gunner and 12 soldiers, and they have to be on guard every other night ; and the castle is useful to Falmouth harbour. And he annexes to his petition a certificate by the master &c. of the Trinity House, that St. Mawes castle is of especial use for the safety of Falmouth harbour, and the fortifying and manning of it is necessary for trade there. The certificate is dated the 29th Sept. 1660.

In 1664, the garrison was established at an expense of 9*l.* 11*s.* per diem, to commence from the 25th day of June, 1664. The particulars of this " establishment" are contained in an entry preserved at the Record Office, (St. Pa. Dom. Ser. [Ent. Book 20. p. 24.] vol. 100. no. 67.), and are as follow :—

		s.	
Two Captains one of y^m to bee Governour } at 8s. each p. diem ... ... }	oo	16	oo
Two lieuten^{ts} each 4s.	oo	o8	oo
Two Ensignes each 3s.	oo	o6	oo
Four Serjeants each 18d.	oo	o6	oo
Six Corparalls each 12d.	oo	o6	oo
Two Drummers each 10d.	oo	o1	8

Two hundred Souldiers each 8d.	06	13	04
Chaplaine	00	05	00
Chirurgien	00	02	6
Two Gunners each 18d.	00	03	00
Three Matrosses each 10d.	00	02	06
Fire & Candles for Guards	00	01	00

09   11   00—p diem.

That was to be the establishment from the 25th June, of the Scilly Isles, of Trusco, and of St. Mawes castle.

The date is July 15th, 1664, and the signatures are as follow :—

ALBEMARLE.
J. SOUTHAMPTON.
HENRY BENNET.

A warrant was issued on the 18th July, 1664, for payment to the governor of 89*l* 17*s*. 6*d*. expended for repairs of the castle. (vol. 100, no. 81.)

A warrant was issued on the 26th May, 1665, for a grant to Viel Vivyan, in reversion after Sir Richard Vivyan, Bart, his father, of the office of captain of the castle. (Clar. St. Pa. vol. 122. no. 49.)

Sir Richard Vyvyan is stated in Burke's Peerage and Baronetage, to have died on the 3rd Oct. 1655. This may be a misprint for 1665. Certainly Sir Richard was living in that year. Not improbably he died before the end of it.

He was succeeded in the governorship by his son, (see Hals in Gilb. vol. 3, p. 134,) Sir Vyel Vyvyan.

Hals relates (in Gilb. vol. 2, p. 277,) that Sir Vyel Vyvyan "was so far imposed upon by John Earl of Bath, by licence of King Charles II., as to sell the inheritence of the lands whereon this castle stands, to him for 500*l*.; who forthwith transferred it over to Sir Joseph Tredinham, Knight, who then became Governor thereof."

Sir Vyel Vyvyan died without issue in the year 1696. (Burke). It may be presumed, that Sir Joseph Tredenham was appointed to the governorship of the castle in that year; and that the transfer to him of the castle lands by the Earl of Bath, did not occur until after the death of Sir Vyel.

It appears probable from a report dated in 1698, which will be mentioned presently, that Sir Joseph Tredenham was still governor up to nearly that date. And I think the statement contained in Hitchins and Drew's history that he was made governor by King Charles II., is as likely to be erroneous as the statement by the same authority that he was displaced at the Revolution of 1688. (Hitch. & Drew, vol. 2, p. 349, and see Lyson, vol. 3, p. 154.)

The deputy governor in Sir Joseph Tredenham's time was Mr. Boscawen.

Sir Joseph Tredenham was displaced from the governorship by King William III., (Hals in Gilb. vol. 2, p. 277; Hitch & Drew, vol. 2, p. 349; Lyson, vol 3, p. 154), presumably in the year 1697, or 1698, and certainly before April, 1698.

He was "succeeded by Hugh Boscawen, Esq., afterwards Lord Falmouth." (Lyson, and see Hitch & Drew, *ubi sup.*)

Sir Joseph Tredenham, after the appointment of his deputy to the governorship, presented a petition to the lords of the Treasury, praying payment of the clearings due to himself, his late deputy and gunners in the castle of St. Mawes; stating what was due, and submitting the matter to their lordships. The earl of Ranelagh made a report dated 16th April, 1698, upon this petition. (St. Pa. Trea. Ser.) In the minute book, vol. 9. p. 47, 21 Dec. 1698, is the following :—"The sum due to Sir Joseph Tredenham & Mr. Boscawen for the garrison of St. Mawes, is to be paid by the Earl of Ranelagh." (Cal. St. Pa. Tr. Ser.)

Hals, who wrote probably about 1719, (he speaks of the government of the castle having been given by King William III. "to his Privy Councillor, the Right Honourable Hugh Boscawen, Esq., now in posession thereof at the writing of these lines"—see Hals in Gilb. vol. 2, p. 277—and Mr. Boscawen was made Viscount Falmouth in 1720), says (in Gilb. vol. 2, pp. 276-7), with reference to St. Mawes castle, "having now about thirty cannon, demy cannon and culverins pertaining thereto (but scarcely so many soldiers of war). The Captain and Keeper whereof hath from the King 54*l*. 15*s*.; his deputy 27*l*. 7*s*. 6*d*.; three Gunners in all 72*l*." As to the fees and the number of soldiers, a comparison of this account with that given for the year 1664 (*vide sup.*), may give rise to some doubt as to the accuracy of Hals' statement.

In 1720, the Right Honourable Hugh Boscawen was created Viscount Falmouth. (Lyson, vol. 3, p. 102.)

He died the 25th Oct. 1734. (Burke).

Lyson says, (vol. 3, p. 154.), that Sir Joseph Tredenham "was displaced, and succeeded by Hugh Boscawen, Esq., afterwards Lord Falmouth, who was removed in 1734, Major de Roen being then appointed by King George II." Lord Falmouth was removed by death in 1734.

Major de Roen succeeded Viscount Falmouth in the governorship in 1734.

Adjutant General Scipio Duroure succeeded Major de Roen in the governorship, but at what exact date I have not ascertained; it may have been about 1740.

Adjutant General Duroure died in 1745. He was buried in Westminster Abbey, and on a monument erected there to his memory is inscribed the following :—

"Scipio Duroure Esqre., Adjutant General of the British Forces, Colonel of the 12th Regiment of Foot and Captain or Keeper of his Majesty's Castle of St. Mawes. He died from wounds received at the battle of Fontenoy, May 10. 1745."

This gallant soldier was succeeded in the governorship of St. Mawes castle by his brother, Lieut. General Alexander Duroure, in 1745 : who retained the governorship probably until his death in 1765. On the same marble on which the memory of his brother is perpetuated in Westminster Abbey, appears the following inscription :—

"And Alexander Duroure Esqre., Lieut. General of the British Forces, Colonel of the 4th or King's own Regiment of Foot, and Captain or Keeper of his Majesty's Castle, of St. Mawes. He died at Toulouse in France after 57 years' faithful service, January 2, 1765."

On the 8th May, 1765, Lieut. General Sir R. Pigot, Bart., was appointed captain or keeper of the castle. He retained this office until his death in 1796. On the 2nd Aug. 1796, Col. Edward Morrison was appointed to the governorship of St. Mawes castle. But on the 2nd of November, of the same year, he was removed to the governorship of Chester. On the 1st Nov. 1796, Field Marshal Sir George Nugent, Bart., G.C.B., was appointed captain or keeper. For all this information I am indebted to the courtesy of the authorities at the war office.

Lyson, writing in 1814, says (vol. 3, p, 154), "The Castle estate is in moieties between the Marquis of Buckingham and James Buller, Esq., M.P."

On the 24th Sept. 1812, during Sir George Nugent's governorship, Major Martin E. Aloes was appointed deputy governor of the castle, the previous deputy governor having died in 1811. Major Aloes was removed to a post in Edinburgh in 1815. On the 18th May, 1815, Lieut. Colonel C. D. Graham was appointed deputy governor. He retained that office until his death, 7th July, 1828. On the 23rd Oct. 1828, Major General Sir Alexander Cameron, K.C.B., was appointed deputy governor. He resigned the office on getting a reward, the 26th April, 1842. The office itself was thereupon abolished. Sir George Nugent retained the captainship until his death, the 11th March, 1849. The office of captain was thereupon abolished. I am much indebted to the authorities at the war office for their courtesy in supplying to me all this information, which I could not easily have obtained without their assistance. Lyson, writing in 1814, (vol. 3, p. 154.) and Drew writing in 1824, (vol. 2, p. 349.), name General Nugent as the governor.

Since the abolition of the offices of governor and deputy governor, there has been no other representative of those ancient officers, than the officer of artillery for the time being having command of the garrison, which I happened to be in the year 1873.